Ghada Dridi is a Tunisian woman and mother. She is an academic deeply interested in global learning and the idea of multiple harmonious belongings. She believes in interconnectivity. Being an officer's daughter, she was influenced by the nature of her father's job.

Ghada experienced instability, developed a sense of flexibility, adaptability, and acceptance from an early age, and realized how enriching 'difference' is. She also holds a Ph.D. in marketing from the University of Tunis El-Manar and is a certified professional coach.

Interestingly, she has taught for nine years at Tunisian universities, and she's the author of scientific articles in the field of her specialization. Also, she was a reading committee member on behalf of the international conferences.

In memory of my father.

For fresh graduates who are looking to make a promising job career.

For people wishing to immigrate and expat – housewives who are looking to integrate into a foreign job market and build up their careers.

For retirees who want to expand their professional experience and allow young people to benefit from their experiences and knowledge.

To ambitious people looking to keep moving, enhancing their conditions despite difficult, unstable, and unexpected circumstances.

Ghada Dridi

Succeeding in Uncertain Times

AUSTIN MACAULEY PUBLISHERS™
LONDON • CAMBRIDGE • NEW YORK • SHARJAH

Copyright © Ghada Dridi 2024

The right of Ghada Dridi to be identified as author of this work has been asserted by the author in accordance with Federal Law No. (7) of UAE, Year 2002, Concerning Copyrights and Neighboring Rights.

All rights reserved. No part of this publication may be reproduced, stored in a retrieval system, or transmitted in any form or by any means, electronic, mechanical, photocopying, recording, or otherwise, without the prior permission of the publishers.

Any person who commits any unauthorized act in relation to this publication may be liable to legal prosecution and civil claims for damages.

The age group that matches the content of the books has been classified according to the age classification system issued by the Ministry of Culture and Youth.

ISBN – 9789948776444 – (Paperback)
ISBN – 9789948776451 – (E-Book)

Application Number: MC-10-01-7323917
Age Classification: E

Printer Name: iPrint Global Ltd
Printer Address: Witchford, England

First Published 2024
AUSTIN MACAULEY PUBLISHERS FZE
Sharjah Publishing City
P.O Box [519201]
Sharjah, UAE
www.austinmacauley.ae
+971 655 95 202

"We learned about gratitude and humility – that so many people had a hand in our success."

– Michelle Obama

I would like to thank my husband for seeing through my vision and supporting me to bring out this book.
Thank you!

I'm grateful for all the expected and unexpected challenges that life puts on my way at every stage of my life, for all circumstances that shaped and reshaped who I am and revealed my hidden sides.

I strongly believe in the power of connecting with each other and that life isn't a matter of fight or winner and loser. Instead, it is a balanced report that allows everyone to live his journey and to support his partner without giving up on his identity, beliefs, and values. Life is not stable, and progress is not linear. The more we support each other, the best will be our journey.

Thank you to my family, friends, and everyone with whom I shared and debated every idea and with whom I connected.

Table Of Contents

Introduction	**11**
The Age Of "Moving Sand"	**17**
1. The "Liquid Uncertain" Times	*19*
2. The Safe Uncertainty: How to Have a Sense of Security Beyond Uncertainty?	*23*
3. The Global System: "One Global System"	*28*
a. Global Citizenship	29
b. Global Education	32
c. The Skills of the Global Citizen	45
d. Rivalries at the Global Level: The Global Labor	53
4. Pivot Career	*66*
5. How to Successfully Make a Change of Direction	*68*
Think In Terms Of Alternatives	**71**
1. Have a Helicopter View	*75*
2. Develop Our Perceptions	*77*
a. It All Starts with Perception	78

b. The Gap Between Perception and Reality	83
c. The Logic of Perception	87
d. Strengthening Our Perceptions	89
e. The Importance of Perceptive Acuity	90
f. The Duality: Seed-Catalyst	92
Think In Terms Of Opportunities	**96**
1. Visualize the Opportunity	*98*
a Uncertainties-Opportunities-Mobility	98
b. Complementarity Between Problem-Opportunity and Solution-Profit	104
c. Perception of Opportunity	105
d. The Attacker's Mindset: Offensive Approach	106
2. Creation of Opportunities	*112*
a. A Dynamic, Positive, and Committed Mindset	113
b. A Good Self-Knowledge	114
c. Being Open to Learning	116
d. Developing One's Visibility and Networking	118
3. Seizing the Opportunities	*119*
a. Looking for Opportunities	120
b. Identifying Opportunities	122
References	**125**

Introduction

How did I come up with this book?

It all started after I moved to Dubai as part of the relocation of my partner! It was a delicate and difficult decision. I had a choice between giving up my job or taking leave without pay. I finally opted for the second alternative. A position for which I had sacrificed years of study and research to prepare a doctoral dissertation in marketing, to succeed in a national competition, to meet the challenges I posed, and to prove myself. But we cannot control everything; circumstances sometimes have the last word. On the other hand, we have the power of reflection to divert them in one's favor and to create opportunities. Of course, it is not easy, but nothing is ever easy!

Once I settled in Dubai, I was really impressed with the work culture. Everyone works and does so with respect for themselves and their profession, regardless of their position, from the simple workforce to the senior officer. Seriousness, attention, and commitment are always present. Of course, they work to earn money, but this attitude allows them to better control what they do, create added value, and above all, improve. I have always asked myself these questions:

How can I find a place in a highly competitive market?

How can I make a difference and create added value?

It is from these questions that I began my new adventure. This questioning attitude has made me think, rethink and rephrase different ideas and situations and even consider achievements. Dubai has given me the opportunity to experience global citizenship, see what a competitive job market is, and learn, shape, and reshape my ideas and perceptions. All I knew was that one never learned enough.

I learned a lot from this country, and my goal was to spread a way of thinking and seeing things.

How to proceed, and where to start?

I did not really have a clear idea. But I knew I wanted to share my thoughts to support anyone facing change. Any woman who, like me, does not want to give up her career and her dream, but on whom family constraints are imposed and who is obligated to make decisions, to assume the consequences, and especially not to get lost along the way.

For I realized that sometimes when circumstances dictate, you just have to adapt and be flexible to carry on your path and pursue your dreams. Some problems cannot be solved; the possible solution is to look at them differently and continue living with them.

I took the time to observe, read, ask myself questions, talk with friends, allow myself to update my knowledge, be open, attend events and conferences, and not stay stuck in the certainty of cause-effect relationships. One relationship does not encourage generative reflection. Instead of generating new opportunities, thinking differently, and using your creative mind, all the attention would be focused on what was done before, past experiences, and ready-made formulas. It is not because we are not compatible with the labor market at any given time that we will be here all our lives!

When you are in a country where different cultures and beliefs, different curricula, practices, experiences, and backgrounds coexist, it can only strengthen our "accountability" and "empowerment" and enrich our reflection. We are responsible for our destiny, our development, and the path to take. Our reflection is our driving force to mobilize and change from one discipline to another to remain in tune with different evolutions and changes, and especially, advance in the haze of uncertainty.

In this book, I started with a number of points that I will share with you:

1. Employment is not necessarily the responsibility of the government.
2. We are not supposed to work systematically and automatically in the same specialty we learned during university studies.
3. Managing our professional career is our responsibility and not that of our employer: you are the author of your story.
4. Evolution does not necessarily follow a linear trajectory: it is about seizing the opportunities available to you rather than just climbing the ladder.

In short, here are three key ideas that must be constantly in mind throughout your reading:

- Uncertainty is a fact;
- Non-linearity is a reality;
- Flexibility is the secret of evolution;

The pace of evolution in this country has made me think of the pace of progress and development that we, as entrepreneurs, job seekers, fresh graduates, and employees, must continuously follow to keep our place in the race. To know what you want is to be aware of yourself, your potential, limits, environment, and the different evolutions and changes taking place. To recognize the path to take is to recognize the direction to follow, to have a clear vision, a well-established strategy, and a well-studied schedule. How to implement everything? How to respond to and manage the unexpected? How can we follow our path and achieve our goals if we are immersed in uncertainty and instability? How can we not lose our selves and disperse in an interconnected and hectic environment?

This book aims to answer these questions by inviting you to rethink different positions and situations and to realize the importance of the relationship that the "how" has with uncertainty, perception, and opportunities.

Just as in chess, you must not stop moving. You must know your own movements and anticipate your opponent's, have the imagination to see the chessboard from above, and decide the next steps. It is necessary to review, have a lot of information and especially knowledge, learn from our successes and failures and those of other players, observe their game well, and analyze their movements to inform us. We need to identify opportunities, wrong steps, and potential ideas. All this is similar to our current life, but ours is much more hectic. Just as in chess, you have to learn to explore the position of pieces, analyze the possible scenarios and then move and embark into the game without knowing for certain your opponent's strategy.

Yes, our life is like a chessboard. We have to study its movements and be prepared for uncertainties. With continuous learning, we will be able to manage the unexpected, solve problems, have out-of-the-ordinary creative ideas, detach ourselves from the center to explore the peripheries, touch areas that might once seem "dark," to visualize our path amid the mist of sand and no longer be afraid of "darkness."

Because the world is changing, because we seek to leave our traces, to improve humanity; because we do not like to play the role of the victim, not to remain at the mercy of the other, nor to spend our time complaining, accusing the educational system and blaming it for our failures, nor to remain passive. Because we are human beings who find fulfillment in the added value they can provide to their society and in the example they will set for future generations. Because we care about the future of our children, grandchildren, and society. Because in the well-being and development of our minds lies the well-being and development of humanity. For all these reasons, we must think constructively. Let us be "out of the box." Let us break free from passively inherited borders and boundaries. Let us accept and encourage differences to broaden our vision and build a better world. A world that can embrace all our differences. Everything happens in the head; it is the reflection that leads us to action.

The Age Of "Moving Sand"

"We are all going to be walking on moving sand," Therefore, "The only way to win is to learn faster than anyone else."

– Zygmunt Baumann
– Eric Ries

The world has always been uncertain, and every era has its own problems and challenges. But the question is, "What has accelerated this change? What has made everything interconnected and interdependent?" It is the new technology. It has changed and altered our perceptions and emotions, our ability to understand what is happening in the world, and our decisions, reactions, and actions (Syrett & Devine, 2012). Thanks to the new technology, we are constantly informed about everything happening around the world's four corners. We can no longer be unconcerned or isolated. We are interested in the impact of the Arab Spring on migratory flows, the price of oil, jobs, and its economic, social, and financial impact, so our perception of stability and certainty is no longer the same.

1. The "Liquid Uncertain" Times

"As we learn about the universe, we gain both a sense of our significance with a vast space and a wonder that feeds thirst of exploration, discovery, and answers to the questions of our existence."

– *Zygmunt Bauman and Tim May*

We live in a time when stability and sedentariness are no longer the norm. The challenges that every person faces are unlimited in number and diverse in nature. Nothing but going from one generation to another, watching your child grow up, and thinking about how to educate them has become a challenge in itself. Nothing is as before, and no one can guarantee or predict, with certainty, future times. This is largely the result of the revolution in information technology, which has impacted the nature of communication. It has taken on a new dimension beyond physical, psychological, and cultural boundaries and barriers. A communication that connects the four corners of the world while integrating the whole of humanity in all its differences.

Mass media is a term that we use when we talk about television…it is a term that stresses the passivity of the receiver of the message. Today, communication has created unprecedented interactivity involving different stakeholders; the advertiser or the person who posts the content, the content creator, and the internet users who will communicate all together and who are scattered and active worldwide. So, you have become exposed to a fairly large flow of information. That is what makes the information available, if not abundant.

The easiest thing to have is information since the internet, social networks, and search engines are available to everyone, and everyone is free to post comments, videos, and content they want to share with the community. It is interactive communication, beneficial interactivity, that connects the whole world and makes it a "Global Village."

The term *"Global village"* is an expression I borrowed from the park located in Dubai. The latter is made up of a wide range of pavilions representing different cultures from different countries, allowing visitors to move from one culture to another; try different cuisines; enjoy the dance performance of one country or another; communicate with others who were considered, in another context, to be foreigners; discover different languages and have fun saying a few words or even a few letters; look at live choreographies performances made in all simplicity, representing the wedding parties or other occasions. By going to the Global Village, the visitor realizes how much cultures are alike in their differences and complement each other in their diversities, that boundaries and barriers are only geographical, and that continuity and openness to others only create new visions and new opportunities. One ends up becoming "a global citizen" of a global village when the citizens of humanity discover each other and explore but do not judge each other, and visitors are hungry to discover differences.

It is a village of coexistence in which we can experience the meaning of "liquid times," where everything meets, everything flows, and nothing stops. Every time we visit a pavilion, test a new cuisine, or admire a new choreography, we find ourselves shaped and reshaped. Each culture leaves an imprint on us. That is how the whole world should be perceived, I think. A mosaic of cultures whose assortment derives its originality from differentiation and whose diversification promotes continuity and development.

Thus, with social networks (Instagram, Facebook, Twitter, Snapchat, etc.), professional networks (LinkedIn), and search engines, interactive communication is set up, and information has become available and accessible. Everyone has the information, but not everyone has knowledge.

In fact, on the university benches, students are looking for knowledge rather than information. They are interested in learning certain skills such as information analysis, in-depth reading, active observation, and broadening perception, which allows them to build and access knowledge and not be content with the coldness and passivity of receiving information. Knowledge alone is not enough because we can have in mind knowledge of different types, theories, and information without knowing how to use them, handle them, process them, and especially how to create links between the different types of knowledge and cast experience in a particular field on another discipline. Mathematics, arithmetic, literature, and other disciplines have become the basis. This will make a difference. What adds value to the young graduate is the skills. To be equipped with thinking and social skills is to have the ability to think effectively, generatively, constructively, creatively, and above all, to manage the time of uncertainty without getting lost in a maze.

Knowledge gives value to information, and skills allow you to better use your knowledge, facilitate your path to success and secure your shoulder. This is what makes career change possible and project entrepreneurship accessible to fresh graduated.

Anyone can have one or more degrees in different disciplines or specialties, but the difference is in skills. Not every teacher is necessarily a good lecturer or researcher, and vice versa. You have to know yourself well to develop and hone your skills.

If we are in the information age, it is because the development of communication techniques has brought radical changes in our daily lives, which has caused a new cultural dimension, namely virtuality. Henceforth, it is no longer a virtual world but a virtual reality. For, virtuality has become a fundamental dimension of our reality, providing us with symbols, icons, and patterns from which we think, perceive, and exist (Castell, 2000). It is a new reality that some will find difficult to adapt and appropriate. In contrast, for others, young or old, it will be part of the normal and the obvious. Accompanied by other technological developments, and economic transformations, we are a network society. Indeed, society is woven from networks as well as social practices, and it is perceived as a network rather than a structure. It is a "random matrix" formed simultaneously by connections and disconnections, containing an unlimited number of possibilities, an infinity of alternatives, and innumerable permutations. It is a society of networks with a flexible, manageable, mobile, and instantaneous character. This new form of society, the network society, marks the transition from the solid phase of modernity to the liquid one. A transition from a rigid phase in which everything is endowed with a single truth, where connections are made in a well-determined direction, according to a predetermined logic, towards a liquid phase. This latter, which supports all possible contradictions, is not afraid of fluidity and does not fear darkness. It is eager to continuously discover and explore to innovate and add value in all fields and disciplines.

But we must be wary of the abundance of information, which will gain ground at the expense of knowledge. We become reservoirs in which information is placed in large numbers, which gives us the illusion of knowing this or that subject when that is not the reality. This liquid phase of modernity requires continuous learning, an open mind, and a wide range of perspectives. As Elif Shafak said, we live in a liquid time and must learn to become intellectual nomads. I think that is the real challenge.

2. The Safe Uncertainty: How to Have a Sense of Security Beyond Uncertainty?

Are you familiar with Maslow's hierarchy of needs?

Security (having shelter, employment, medical security, etc.) is the second need to be met after physiological needs (eating, drinking, sleeping, etc.). It is about physical, emotional, and psychological security, the presence of trust, and refraining from judging others. Once we are safe, our impulsiveness diminishes. Our state of mind changes as we move forward to meet our needs, to achieve an interdependent mindful state, in which we will seek our sense of life: what do we want to accomplish? We ask ourselves what are the different means we have, our assets, our strengths, and our weaknesses, especially if we are open to the world, each other, differences, changes, and unforeseen events. We are beyond the spirit of independence in which we have proven ourselves. We evaluated and discovered ourselves to look for interference. We are aware that interdependence is a great way to move forward and improve. The world is interconnected; everything and every event take the form of a flow, a stream of water that has no limits, that can take different forms, and whose speed is unstable. It would be interesting to collaborate, forge new alliances, learn from others, and enrich one's networking to navigate safely in fickle currents of water. We are safe because we are all equipped, know how to ask for help when necessary, and most importantly, have our network and built our image within our community, so we are not a lambda, but we have our trustworthiness account. This is what will encourage others to collaborate with us, help us, guide us, and especially believe in us. We don't invest in a team that has no potential, do we? On the other hand, we invest in a losing team if it is promising.

Two factors allow the feeling of security to take place:

- **The clarity of intent**: this implies clarity of vision, an awareness of our objectives, of ourselves (of our values, our potentials, and our interferences), and of circumstances. Better self-management allows you to assume yourself, be authentic and flexible, and maintain your positivity.
- **Trust the "process"**: this implies, on the one hand, a social conscience: no judgment but rather an interest in exploring, being curious, asking questions, and better managing relationships by trusting the other, working together, and meeting challenges. On the other hand, a knowledge of our objectives: what we want to achieve, and breaking down this objective into a series of steps to pursue one's vision and not get lost along the way.

When we know what we want, we become aware of the skills and means at our disposal, we understand the demands of the market, and we visualize the position we can take if we work on ourselves and be open to others. That's when security takes place. You will be able to face uncertainty and not tell stories, anticipate and assess future risks and changes, and visualize the different paths to take.

Once safe, piloting it will be easier. We are only responsible for managing the unexpected and the changes that will occur along the way. For the rest, our safety is already assured.

It is the safety of uncertainty. If safety is a need, a real need, certainty is not; it is not part of Maslow's hierarchy of needs. Indeed, if security is associated with certainty, it implies the control of the various factors, conditions, and changes based on our knowledge and achievements, which is impossible. We cannot control technological development, changing people's mindsets, ambitions, and market trends. Therefore, we will always be disappointed with what life offers and surprised at things that do not correspond to the ideas we have always believed in. We must be aware that we are developing our professional careers and personal relationships and creating our network in a context of uncertainty. In fact, uncertainty is the only certainty. By satisfying our security needs, we can move forward and prosper in uncertainty.

Uncertainty is about integrating an entrepreneurial, open, risk-taking mindset that embraces change, is receptive to different meanings and perspectives, is not limited to what is gained, and leaves room for experimentation and exploration. We are in liquid times where we must constantly rethink our habits and not over-analyze ideas and situations. Instead, we must move forward at our own pace, savoring small achievements, which will improve our skills and performance and allow us to overcome the various obstacles (internal and external) that we may encounter along the way.

Thus, the security of uncertainty is:

- **A zone of adventure** that allows us to push our limits, develop our curiosity, explore new perspectives and new horizons safely, exploit the different learning to develop, and see life as a source of learning, not of problems. Although "adventure" and "security" seem contradictory, in my opinion, their arrangement is possible. We are safe because we have confidence in the process and a vision and objectives that are measurable, feasible, and realistic.
- **A framework for reflection** in which we wear several hats, take different angles of vision, know exactly where we are going, have confidence in the process, and are constantly on the move. When the solutions are not good and do not solve everything, we must recognize them! You have to know how to manage even when the visibility and the infrastructure are not good.
- **An ever-changing,** mobile, and flexible mindset that does not tolerate generalities (my reality, views, beliefs, and perceptions are not everyone's) and allows us to become familiar with the changes. We must always challenge and update our skills and knowledge. When unexpected things occur, ask

questions and explore meaning instead of sinking into judgments and searching for pretexts and arguments.

Why Too Much Analysis Hinders Our Development?

An analysis is indispensable for understanding a situation because we manage to understand a subject in terms of what we already know by using the models of thought we have already experienced and acquired from past experiences. If faced with a new situation, person, or problem, we will first try to recognize it, identify it and see what we know about it. If it is always new and complex, we will break down the situation into parts that are easy to recognize and handle, analyze them, and then formulate the whole image and have an analysis of the entire situation. Such an analysis will make it possible to identify the causes, understand what happened, and take the necessary actions. But sometimes, even if we manage to know the cause of the problem, we cannot do anything about it, neither eliminate it nor find a solution; these are problems that will be part of our life or even sometimes of our daily life. In this sense, the analysis will not be able to solve this type of problem. Such problems do not need analysis but rather a new approach and design. In this sense, the analysis lacks creativity and design because we always remain conditioned by past experiences and by what we know. At the same time, we need new conceptions, designs, and perceptions to move forward and continue our journey.

3. The Global System: "One Global System"

"Why roots were rated so highly compared with branches or leaves...Trees had multiple shoots and filaments extending in every direction, under and above the ancient soils of the earth. If even roots refused to stay put, why expecting the impossible from human being."

– Elif Shafak

In liquid times, we find ourselves caught in flows and currents of information, which we must know, read and analyze. These flows make this world "one global system" (Castel, 2010), where everything is connected, nothing is dissociated, and what happens in one country can impact another at the other end of the world. A new technology, a new approach. Everything is spreading and affecting different fields and different specialties. Thus, the world has become a global system in which companies, universities, financial markets, students, recruiters, engineers, doctors, and patients...are all connected in a network society operating on a global scale anchored in the same network. Nothing is more immune to globalization; even education, skills, and knowledge take advantage of their global character.

The entire Earth is criss-crossed by streams of information that are interwoven. It is a global system in which information, places, and people are relatively accessible. The most remote places and physical distance are no longer a constraint. Wherever you are, everything is almost affordable.

The world has become an interconnected system, culturally and socially, through travel, study internships abroad, expatriation, migration, and social networks, economically through international trade, and politically through international relations.

This global system has created two equally important concepts; global citizenship and global worker. It is about a new structure of citizenship and labor market. Hence, the importance of "global education."

a. Global Citizenship

In these modern times, citizenship in its most classical sense is no longer appropriate. Nowadays, we are no longer part of a single country or nation, a unique culture, spirit, or know-how. It is rather a question of "multiple belonging" that is rich in experiences and tastes and broad in its references. This global system has established multiculturalism at the center of the dynamism of the multicultural network society, whose virtual world is the new reality.

Coming from one country, we live in another one, even several, we grow up in another, work and get settled in a third, learn different languages, explore different cultures, experience different cuisines, frequent different nationalities, travel, read. Each one of us is a mosaic of "belongings." It is in this sense that we speak of global citizenship. We are exposed to all the possible and imaginable differences. We are impacted by all the cultures we had the chance to discover either by reading, by documentaries or by what we one day have been part of. We reflect, think, and analyze in different ways. Multiple belongings are an attitude and a state of mind that make us open to the world around us and like to observe and take a different look, which changes the angle of vision each time a new challenge arises. It makes us a person who is afraid neither of the stranger nor of the non-common and who does not seek clash but rather the discovery of the other, of the culture, and of new perspectives. It is someone who finds their comfort in movement and not in stagnation, reflection and not in dogmatism, effort and not in laziness, accountability and not in victimization.

What seems familiar to us and what best fits into a well-defined cultural framework or in a particular public or digital space may be foreign to another culture or space. Therefore, the multiculturalism that gives us this multiple belonging gives us the ability to interact with strangers with ease while welcoming their differences and without leaving them imprisoned in their own culture. This allows us to explore the other, broaden our perceptions, and realize that a single truth is no longer welcome in a world of networks in which we are all strangers. Each one carries in himself one's own different assets. It is about thinking of the other in fluid rather than solid terms, letting the difference spread to improve and innovate what exists and connect more to a world of networks. The difference in the background of each of us is an opportunity to make our shared space fruitful and universal by appreciating at best and valuing our humanity, whose richness lies in the difference.

This diversity of belonging in terms of culture, background, trajectory, and experience shapes our perceptions, viewpoints, and receptivity. It frees us from the pieces of evidence and bipolarities that only widen the gaps. Being placed in a box and getting adjusted to it simply rejects and denies our reality which lies in diversification, acceptance, and exploration to highlight the imagination, innovation, and liberation of our minds.

Globalization places multiculturalism and multiple belongings at the heart of social dynamics. A global citizen is a determined citizen with the will to cooperate and learn continuously. He does not seek confrontation but rather conciliation. He adopts a global approach to learning and teaching to put in place fresh graduated who will be qualified to work on a global scale. A global citizen knows well that the world is changing rapidly but also that he can make a difference by the actions he can take, by the empathy that does not leave him indifferent towards the misfortunes of others, by the education that will enrich his mind, by the values that allow him to have a solid foundation and to respect those of others.

In this sense, a global citizen is a conscientious and committed citizen who feels concerned by the various issues, whether local and specific to his country or related to other nations, while remaining connected to his own society, community, and culture. It is about keeping one's roots deeply-anchored and multiplying the branches. He embraces a spirit of inclusion that embraces and not excludes, builds relationships, and does not break them.

There is no parallel world; there is only one in which to coexist. The key element for a global citizen is exploration and respect for differences. It is interested in exploring what connects cultures, communities, and markets…how to grow and add value to their differences, learn new skills and ways of thinking, and free oneself from prejudices and judgments. Rather, it must have the flexibility to benefit from the changes that are taking place in the world as a whole. It forms its own personal identity, which is flexible and multiple. This identity carries within it our cultural heritage in the broad sense of the word, what we have learned, read, and experienced, and all we have appropriated. This global identity does not leave us as aliens disconnected from everything different from us. It opens horizons of learning, development, and improvement. It is no longer an obstacle to the exploration and discovery of the world but rather an advantage that allows us to be confident and prosper in a world in full motion, whose diversification is the main characteristic. This is how today's child, a future global citizen, would be able to face different challenges and stereotypes and not force itself to adjust to a pre-established framework, a framework set by minds that do not accept evolution for fear of change and love for the security that stability provides.

A global citizen is, therefore, one who can look at the world around him broadly and holistically, tries to understand it, and manages to locate himself in it. A global citizen always finds his benchmarks. Changing countries or cultures is not an obstacle but a new opportunity open to him. He is flexible, always takes the lead, and actively participates in his community.

b. Global Education

Suppose we are in the liquid phase of modernity. In that case, this implies a society of networks of instantaneous and flexible character containing many permutations and changes. Thus, the quality of society depends on the quality of its members. They are the ones who will make their society a space for value creation, innovation, improvement, learning, progression, and sharing of knowledge and experience. Suppose education is to be of great importance and continually updated. In that case, it is because it plays a decisive and very important role in the quality of tomorrow's society. How can we be content to teach generations and generations in the same way when we live in a time that is in motion and whose standards are no longer the same? It is in this sense that education is no longer limited to the formal nature, in the sense of school education and the learning of knowledge and information, but also to the informal sense, which contains learning from experience, activities, participation in associations and organizations, the sharing of personal experiences, which will allow to develop skills, to join the theoretical with the practice, to visualize the gaps that can arise, to learn to think, to argue effectively and operationally, and above all, to be aware of the diversity and plurality of points of view. While traditionally education has focused primarily on argumentation and analysis, we need a practical, simple, and time-saving education in this era of information and uncertainty. We need thinking and building skills and generation rather than just criticism.

Learning to be a global citizen is a discipline whose practice begins at school or even at four. We will learn and succeed in it the day when our perception will be flexible and broad. We will become aware of the importance of diversification and the role that union and cooperation can play in improving personal and collective well-being, whether in the family, in the class, in the company, in the country, or around the world. The truth is none other than an organization, a structuring, a well-determined arrangement, which each person makes according to their own perception of facts and conditions. It is multiple and not unique. It is relative to each person and is not necessarily general. Each person is the hero of their own story.

Traditionally, education is limited to analysis, description, understanding, and at best critical thinking. However, this is insufficient, just like a half-finished product, halfway between ignorance and knowledge. Thus, particular attention should be paid to the capacity for reflection. Yes, we must learn to think constructively, creatively, innovatively, critically, and generatively to add value and lead to operational and effective results. What is missing from traditional education is thinking skills. Think about the meaning of effectiveness rather than in terms of analysis and argumentation. In this sense, reading, mathematics, science, writing, and knowledge have become basic and necessary skills that will allow anyone to survive and find a place in a specific market. This is appropriate for the solid phase of modernity. In a society of networks, if we want sustainability, continuity, evolution, and permutation, it is imperative to have thinking skills, social skills, and an understanding of how society works. This is what will make a difference and bring value. Traditional education provides us with literature (reading, writing, and computation), digitalization, and algebra. But, nowadays, we need the skills and the operational thinking.

The key subject of modern education is "reflection." The pivot in times of uncertainty will allow the learner not to get stuck but rather to explore different paths to decide future actions. A pivot mindset is just like the basketball one.

To think is to connect information, knowledge, and experiences to perceive differently, to identify the hidden value, to ask questions, and not to be limited to a pre-established framework. Learning through an interdisciplinary approach allows students to practice and experiment with reasoning. Understanding society implies understanding the functioning and interaction between events and actions that take place and form our society and our perception of the world as a whole.

Therefore, the appropriate education for a global citizen should focus on critical and creative thinking, communication, and the ability to think and analyze. It should not consist in dictating or telling him what they must do, but rather in arming them with knowledge, values, and skills enabling them to challenge the various uncertainties and not to fear them, to make the most appropriate decisions for the most critical situations and to assume one's responsibilities, while taking into account the consequences that this may entail. It is an education that helps learners make their own choices through a critical analysis and evaluation of the different options that present themselves and the implications of their choice. This is how this young child, a future global citizen, will formulate a well-established understanding of global citizenship. Thus, the school, college, or university must be the center of learning global citizenship. From there, the learner, from a young age, realizes the diversity and realizes that the family environment with its values, cultures, and background is nothing but one node among others. He also learns that diversity does not mean negating oneself, denying one's origins, and not judging does not mean being indifferent. At school, in large part, he makes sense of things to know the limits of each of the attributes of global citizenship because it is over there that an opportunity is offered to practice global citizenship and explore the world. At this moment, we start, teachers and parents, to save our children from extremism to enlighten their minds, and to put aside all kinds of discrimination in favor of the added value that diversification and the multitude of identities we can have would provide.

Continuity is not limited to the conservation of traditional heritage but rather involves improvement, adaptation, and synchronization. Suppose the world changes its character, giving up stability in favor of uncertainty. In that case, we must reconsider the subject taught and put it forward to our students, the future global citizens. With the development of technology, information has become accessible to everyone. Therefore, advancing knowledge to the learner is important but not enough. He needs to be equipped with skills with a high degree of fluency in their practice to be comfortable with the processing and manipulating of information and knowledge learned at school, university, and in his own experiences.

Thus, the aim of education would be to develop a sense of criticism and proactivity in the learner. He must be able to take a critical look at all types of problems, opportunities, and challenges but also be agile, active, and proactive to react, take the necessary measures, adapt to opportunities and unleash creativity, and above all, think laterally; a way to move from the center and explore peripherals. That will make a difference and create added value on an ongoing basis.

Knowledge will allow us to better understand, but understanding itself does not allow us to move forward and improve. The capacity for reflection will make it possible to create value, follow the rhythm, and be in phase with liquid times. Education teaches the learner effectiveness. It is not just about criticism; it is about finding new ideas and designs. It is not just a matter of analyzing but of understanding the causes and the impact. To be effective is to learn to think flexibly and free oneself from the rigidity of certain rules and instructions. It ensures continuity in an uncertain environment.

Suppose the world is interconnected, interdependent and in constant motion. In that case, education should be able to keep pace and speed, not get stuck in old clichés, but evolve and adapt to the new reality, such as virtual reality and the liquid nature of modern times. This will be possible only if the learner becomes comfortable with critical thinking but also when they actively engage in society. This will allow them to seize, identify, and anticipate opportunities, failures, and possible solutions. Thus, education must make it possible to develop the knowledge and understandings, skills, values, and attitudes that every learner would need to integrate into a global society and economy, to prepare global workers who do not fear the change from one labor market to another but who still find an opportunity. Because they know well that it is these opportunities that will allow them to develop their skills.

The mapping of interconnectivity and global interdependence

As we move forward in education and the idea of global citizenship is developed, it must be reflected in school education. The function of the school is to ensure synchronization with today's world. It is about nurturing young minds, cultivating them, and developing their skills to prepare future leaders, future thinkers, and citizens of tomorrow who are familiar with the idea of global citizenship and who seek to develop and continuously improve it. If the world is a globally interconnected and interdependent system, this should be reflected in the modules taught to students. For example, according to IHS Markit, the URI snowstorm that hit Texas in February 2021 impacted the oil production of the United States, which led to a worldwide rupture of raw materials such as resin. As a result, prices of petroleum derivatives such as plastic have skyrocketed.

To be prepared for a global labor market and acquire the necessary knowledge and diplomas, one must be first educated and have a solid foundation to pivot and score goals. It is in this sense that an interdisciplinary approach is required. If the world is criss-crossed with links, so should be the disciplines taught and the student's perception. From here, the consciousness of the interconnectivity of our world will be built in the child's mind. By creating links between literature, science, mathematics, art, philosophy, and history…the child begins to perceive things on a large scale, prompting him to reflect on what happened, what he is currently experiencing, and what could happen in the future. He becomes familiar with the idea of the global system because he has detached himself from the abstract nature of teaching and is involved in real facts that best concretize this networking.

This mapping resides, for instance, in exploring science through literature by teaching a child to discover the animal world by reading a small story, then allowing him to live an experience by taking him to the zoo or by getting in touch with this animal and exploring it. Therefore, reading is not only about telling stories of unreal fairies but also introduces us to other disciplines, forging our perception and our knowledge. From a young age, this child will learn to ask questions, give his opinion, and especially listen to the opinion of others. Similarly, by reading a story related to robotics, the student then visualizes what he has just read, which allows him to discuss the mechanical characteristics and functionality of a machine to propose simpler instructions for use, and this will encourage him to reflect on the design process to bring new ideas. This is how the links are forged between the different disciplines, literature, sciences, art, history, etc. When taught from real data, even statistics and mathematics allow an intersection between history, statistics, and culture.

Active learning is required by involving action and collaboration with each other. The teacher will deal with an active and participatory class in which he will play the role of facilitator, organizer, and moderator. He organizes the information and knowledge gained by the students. It is about building holistic learning that touches on knowledge, skills, values, and attitudes. It is a global learning that reflects the interconnectedness of today's world but is, above all, in tune with the liquid nature of modern times.

Therefore, the student would be increasingly involved in global problems, explore, and always process the information with more depth. It would be even interesting to teach statistics from a real case study that deals with the percentages of children's school enrolment in a country or a region, discuss the causes and the impact that there can be on a small and large scale, propose solutions…feel involved. This is how we motivate our young people and transmit to them the desire for knowledge, and this is how we prepare our children for global citizenship, which can only be beneficial for everyone, that does not seek to exclude but rather to connect the different pieces, examine the different falls and sources, make this world a planet where there is room for all.

Once the student is involved in his learning, he will be prepared to participate in social and community life, even on a global scale. He learns to be active, reactive, and proactive. He becomes responsible for his decisions and therefore develops his self-esteem. The responsibility and involvement of learning allow the student to take the lead and start his way. He will know what skills need to be developed and what opportunities will enable him to develop his skills, learn and prove himself; hence, the importance of participating in internships, organizations, and voluntary actions. This is individualized learning, where students must design their education and learning.

In this sense, students learn to collaborate and cooperate. They connect their learning. By working together and sharing information, experiences, and knowledge, they will be able to explore the subject in question better. They become responsible for their learning. They participate in formulating the information. They are active stakeholders, as a global citizen should be.

c. At the university

Similarly, in university, teaching must not be content and limited to the search for truth and the right answer. From the moment we live in liquid and uncertain times, in which orientations, preferences, and conditions of all kinds can change from one minute to the next, it would be impossible to be satisfied with a truth that would not bear criticism, questioning, which would be frozen and stable. We need to free ourselves from the obsession with the truth. There is no single solution or opinion; everything can support the diversity and multiplicity of readings.

Traditionally, the university's main mission is to provide the student with knowledge of past experiences and wisdom (De Bone, 2009). In the information age, students do not need the university to access information and knowledge. This is why universities are obliged to teach the skills to their students; otherwise. they will give them training that is out-of-phase with the reality of the market. The university would be considered just as a mandatory passage to graduation and not as a learning center. Thus, a student must be able to think in terms of possibilities and not be a prisoner of a single answer or solution. This is why university studies must consider the current state of affairs and the economic, financial, or labor market and emphasize the practical and effective nature of learning. There must not be a gap between what is taught and the reality of the market. It would be interesting to teach about the economic crisis of 1929 and 2008. But it would be more interesting if the student proposed new solutions, anticipated the types of crises we may be expected to, and studied the change in investor behavior. Accordingly, a student must understand the past through the acquired knowledge. But the most important thing is to design the future. Being endowed with skills, creative thinking, and criticism makes it possible to open horizons without getting stuck in the old tracks.

We need perceptual reasoning to broaden the field of vision, critical reasoning to question ourselves, creative reasoning to create added value, and design thinking to achieve the added value we want.

According to De Bono, the university needs to pay particular attention to four types of skills and teach them to its students while considering their fields of study and future professions. These informational skills allow them to access information from different sources; they are thinking, social and professional skills. In this way, the university will train students to become global citizens "in tune" with the market, who, like liquid times, move seamlessly from one position to another and from one country to another because they have the skills to constantly evolve and explore.

- **Teaching/education:**

There is no single solution or opinion. Everything must support diversity and multiplicity. Also, the motivation for education should not be based on, and limited to, the fact being right. Being right or suggesting the right answer is a one-time thing. We are right at one point in time. If our perception of things changes, we will propose another answer in which we will see ourselves to be right. The most important thing is not to be right or to propose the right answer but rather to be able to criticize, propose new alternatives, generate added value, and to be able to implement them. The most important thing is continuity and sustainability.

We are in a time of active nature. The one who will stand out and succeed is not the one who is right or has proposed the right answer but rather the one who is endowed with the ability to think fluidly and adapt to opportunities.

Therefore, the student must be able to think in terms of possibilities and not be obsessed with a single answer or solution. This is why education must take into account the current state of things and of the market, whether it be labor, economic, or financial, and emphasize the practical and effective nature of learning. There must not be a gap between the theories and approaches taught and the reality of the market.

What is the point of learning the formula and testing the student's ability to manually calculate the psychological price when professional software exists? Isn't it better to know the software, master it and interpret the results and their components?

It is important to teach about the 2008 crisis. But it would be more interesting to know how it is different from previous crises, its impact on some markets such as construction or the automobile, to address the interconnectivity of markets and institutions and to highlight the global nature of our new reality, which has caused different countries to be affected by this health crisis, COVID. Understanding a given problem or situation is important but not enough. Knowledge allows us to understand but to ensure improvement and progression, meet the challenges that arise continuously, and adapt to the opportunities, it would be imperative to think and proceed in terms of possibilities and alternatives to generate new ideas. This is when the need for thinking skills arises. We need to be able to identify and perceive value in everything, whether positive or negative, beneficial or harmful. Creativity is identifying and pointing to value. The more creative one is the one who can see and perceive what has escaped others. Value is the motto of creativity that takes its meaning and importance the more it advances. Therefore, to achieve this, we must have perceptual reasoning to approach a single subject from different angles and critical reasoning to question ourselves, from conceptual reasoning to put the value we have identified into place. We need to understand the past through the knowledge gained, but the most important thing is to design the future.

- **Ingredients and skills**

If global education is the necessary training for a global citizen, this would also apply to the teacher. They should be endowed with this global character; wherever a teacher is, he must be qualified to teach. It is not a question of mastering the subjects to be taught but rather of making this connection between the different teaching approaches while setting up the different thinking skills. Thus, as already stated in De Bono (2017), the teacher's choice and contribution would be decisive, not only in terms of their specialty in the subjects taught but also, and largely in terms of their qualifications as a teacher.

- **Standardized tests**

The liquid and uncertain nature of liquid times, the global character, and the interconnectivity of our world lead us to think of the means of evaluation of learners, pupils, and students. Exams allow us to test our knowledge of the information. It is a way to determine if you know what you should know and learn at school or university. It leaves no room for reflection. So, the exam is very useful and a great way to test knowledge, but it is not enough. It should also test the learner's thinking skills and competencies. The purpose of tests and exams is to prepare the student to bring value, improve and develop the world. It is not a matter of leaving him imprisoned in a curriculum that will handicap his movement in a global system where everything is connected and interdependent. By identifying the skills that will be useful in their progress and development and those that they master best, the learners would be more attentive, careful, and aware of the opportunities that present themselves. They especially would know what opportunity will allow them to develop their best competencies.

The objective of tests or examinations is to prepare the learner to be part of society and the world and bring value to it.

d. The Skills of the Global Citizen

Whether you are an adult or young, you must not get lost in the various cracks but rather keep a healthy mind that allows you to see clearly and have the ability to adapt and be flexible to new developments. Therefore, opportunities and challenges are the two sides of the same coin. The world is changing and progressing at an increasing and rapid rate, and everyone is going to try to make sense of this world that it is not stable. Everyone will have to seize the opportunities to evolve and progress but also face the challenges that arise and meet them to prove to oneself and others, whether they are future recruiters or professional networks. The ability to think, process information, be flexible, creative, and manage change, and these skills will make us unique and original. In an interconnected and interdependent world, we are an integral part of the "global" nature of an event, an action, or an issue. Everything propagates and spreads, and nothing remains specific to a limited space or time. We are one of several nodes in a global and international network, a node connected to different social and professional networks, cultures, organizations, and communities.

The liquid nature of modern times implies the importance of skills: knowing how to swim allows you to swim in calm waters and manage your breathing and your fears; managing your energy allows you to swim in murky streams and go further.

- **Managing uncertainties and complex situations**

A global citizen is a citizen who is aware of the interconnectedness and interdependence of the relationships that shape our world and whose uncertainty stems from the constant change in those relationships. This connection concerns both problems and agreements. Exploring the different connections allows for leeway in the actions to undertake but, above all, to have knowledge allowing to predict and repair the risks that may arise. By exploring the links between different problems and situations, it would be possible to predict future movements and actions to be undertaken. Henceforth, a global citizen is supposed to be increasingly attentive to his direct and indirect environment and able to identify the links between different subjects, to be aware that this interconnectivity implies the concept of mobility that characterizes liquid times. Nothing is dissociated; everything is connected. This must be taken into account in education and learning to prepare a "global labor" capable of working in different conditions, in different cultures, and capable of moving smoothly to adapt to different opportunities regardless of the uncertainties that may appear from one minute to the next. The real limitation of this "global labor" is no longer a curriculum or a diploma but rather a lack of will and curiosity. A global citizen responsible for his learning knows well that the skills at his disposal will allow him to manage uncertainties as well as possible. Suppose he has not followed a curriculum that takes into account the uncertain and liquid nature of modern times. In that case, he will not be afraid to become a nomadic intellectual who seeks the knowledge and skills necessary for his evolution to develop and value them.

In this sense, a global citizen is one who is endowed with a set of skills allowing him a connection to different concerns and a closeness to the different global issues and problems. He should be able to adapt to new circumstances and not get stuck in predetermined paths. He should explore new perspectives and alternatives and not confine himself to a specific framework. Finally, he should be able to anticipate obstacles and uncertainties and think in terms of possibilities. Therefore, mobility and agility are required in an uncertain time invaded by information and whose knowledge and skills will be the key value to succeed and manage the future.

- **Creativity and innovation are the only permanent things.**

Any attempt at transformation, learning, and process of change begins with questions. By asking themselves questions and formulating their own queries, the learners will appropriate their learning and feel more and more concerned and aware of the world around them and that of others which may converge or diverge from their own. By asking ourselves, we learn to structure our questions to better explore and examine a subject from different economic, social, political, and ecological angles. This allows us to connect the local to the global to examine our own hypotheses. Above all, this pushes us to do research, learn, search for information, and then analyze and evaluate it, giving rise to knowledge. Thus, we would no longer be mere reservoirs of information whose receptivity is passive.

On the contrary, each question asked gives rise to one or more pieces of information that will be processed and from which other questions and information may emerge. Hence, links between different subjects are created, and we will become aware of the interconnectivity of the world as a result of the interdependence of its subjects. This will solicit our attention and encourage us to explore more the causes, the consequences, and the extent of a particular problem, to make an effort to criticize the existing solutions and especially to propose new issues, create and come out with new solutions.

In this sense, we must have an open mind that is not limited to judgment and is not afraid to ask questions, criticize and give birth to new ideas. It is important to know that criticism is indispensable in that it allows us to question and explore grey areas but does not allow us to provide answers or alternatives. By being creative, we can imagine, propose a plethora of ideas and alternatives, and use different approaches to solve the same problem.

- **Proactive and agile**

In a turbulent and uncertain environment, it is imperative to keep an eye out and actively process any type of information. This should be done by anyone, regardless of their status and professional experience. Being on standby allows for proactivity and agility.

Proactivity allows us to take the initiative, not to limit ourselves to responding to a situation but rather to anticipate, think in terms of possibilities, and be prepared for different scenarios. This requires a certain degree of decision-making autonomy and accountability for the choices and decisions taken, which will save time and ground. Agility makes it possible to move more quickly and achieve performance. In liquid and uncertain times, nothing can stand stagnation. So, the more we can change direction and/ or strategies in uncertain conditions, the more we can compete with our rivals to identify and spot opportunities. Hence, agility is invaluable, especially in turbulent markets. The more agile and responsive we are, the more we can adapt and seize opportunities. This is why it is imperative to have an entrepreneurial spirit ready to take risks, adapt to changing circumstances, and be comfortable with the uncertainty of modern times (Syrett and Devine, 2012). Moreover, agility has become a criterion of competition; those who are more agile will gain more ground and increase their chances.

In this sense, a global citizen must be provided with the means to bring about positive change and engage in its actions. The idea is not to limit ourselves to information but to seek knowledge to make well-thought-out choices, have well-illuminated visions, and above all, have the will to add value. As a result, the education of a global citizen makes it possible to provide a critical assessment of the various options that present themselves and highlight the implications that emanate from them. A global citizen should be able to do the "mind map," connecting different ideas and concepts to plan in a time of uncertainty. To make our agility operational, we need to look at the short-term visions and the next steps, which will put in place the flexibility and the ability to adapt in time.

We should be able to act quickly and be flexible in the face of unforeseen events and changes, as well as to shape and adapt to opportunities and problems arising from uncertainty (Syrett and Devine, 2012). This also allows us to be tactful and diplomatic, communicate correctly, effectively, and at the right time, share experiences, find compromises, and arrive at beneficial solutions for various parties.

> **Agility = Rapidity + Flexibility**

- **Empathy and self-knowledge**

Our interpretation of the world around us, events, problems, and actions largely depends on our experiences, culture, and values. Our perceptions and perspectives allow us to interpret in one way or another. Thus, to comprehensively understand the different aspects of a given problem or situation, it would be interesting to explore the different perspectives and points of view. However, to explore others' views and values, one must know oneself well and be aware of our own values, limitations, proposals, and assumptions. This is how our ability to communicate would be more and more effective, how we would be able to listen to each other, to argue without aggression, to understand, and above all, to respect diversity. At this point, empathy takes place, fits in our daily lives, and points out that our interest is no longer limited to similarities but also makes us feel empathy for those different from us. We become aware of the fact that accepting difference does not mean adapting and appropriating it, but rather understanding it without judging it. That is how we will make a world where there is room for everyone. In knowing ourselves, we become aware of our identity, values, differences with others, and the wealth diversification can bring.

Liquid times have established an interdependent and interconnected global system in which all things converge. Thus, a global citizen must become aware of himself to the same degree as he knows the others. There is no longer "me and the other;" if we are part of the same matrix, it is because each is responsible for himself and the impact he can have on the other. In this sense, clash, confrontation, and disputes are no longer the best means of accepting differences, finding compromises, and uniting peoples, because they no longer leave room for exploration and only underline differences while burying similarities and complementariness. Therefore, there will be no continuity.

Self-knowledge implies a knowledge of what we know but also of what we do not know, being aware that our knowledge of things is largely impacted by our perception. In this sense, an evaluation of learning is necessary. This evaluation can be made with the learner to develop in him the responsibility for learning. In this way, he will become aware of what he has learned about himself, his points of view, his approach to the subjects, his arguments, and his sense of listening, sharing, and tolerance, but also of what he has learned about the world in general, on certain specific problems.

He must also be aware of the skills he has developed and those he wishes to improve in the future. By assessing ourselves, we will be aware of our progress and the impact that learning will have on our attitudes, behaviors, and future actions. By knowing ourselves, we become aware of our weaknesses and strengths. We can look outward at our actions and thoughts, identify internal obstacles, and work on ourselves without pretending to hold the truth.

This allows us to reflect deeply and clarify future decisions after evaluating the different experiences and learning. We must not have a mind conditioned by inherited cultural and social contexts. But we must allow ourselves to question certain values to clarify and analyze them to determine their impact on future decisions.

We realize that everything is relative and that our complementarity comes from our differences. Thus, we no longer fear the others but discover them. We do not offend but explore the points of view and the reasoning behind them. In interconnectedness and interdependence, empathy takes hold, making us understand the danger and impact of discrimination and judgment on others. We must be aware that different cultures and backgrounds affect our actions and ways of seeing things; hence, perception is important to broaden our perspectives and have a rather rich and free mind.

d. Rivalries at the Global Level: The Global Labor

"We have learned to steer when moving slowly. Now we must learn to race."

– Eric Reis

Working in modern times, characterized by a network society and the interdependence of its various components, implies a rather original mix. It is about having the ability to work alone while forming one's own network while being a relational worker who builds relationships, succeeds in compromises, and always finds common ground. If diversity is a fact, interdependence is imperative to make the world work. To move forward and above all, to ensure sustainable development, entrepreneurship is a new form of individualization. It is not a matter of being removed but rather of being made responsible. You have to be responsible for learning, managing your career, creating networking, and developing the network. This applies both at the personal and professional levels. In this sense, individualization imposes accountability, which excludes victimization.

Traditionally, using and applying a set of powerful and reliable analytical tools make it possible to predict and anticipate the future with enough accuracy and certainty. This makes it possible to take a clear and linear strategic direction corresponding to a well-defined vision. But is this valid and effective when it comes to an uncertain environment where everything is interdependent and interconnected and where the speed of change is very high?

- **Undertake your career**

A professional career is a long journey of learning and perseverance. If innovation is the only permanent thing of modern times, change is the only constant variable of these uncertain times. Everything changes and grows at an incredible speed. Whether it is alliances, new technologies, relationships, perceptions, ways of thinking, the global economy, marketing, medicine, or education, everything without exception is subject to change, development, improvement, and even abandonment. Hence, the growing interest in entrepreneurs who are indispensable for any society whose prosperity and development depend on innovation and creation. In this sense, Ries (2011) defines the entrepreneur as anyone who operates under extreme uncertainty and instability and continually seeks to create value. Moreover, he believes that "entrepreneur" should be considered "a job title" in modern firms whose growth and development depend on innovation. That said, entrepreneurship does not exclude people who work in conditions of stability and security because, from the moment they take care to innovate, improve, create, and seize opportunities, they, in turn, are entrepreneurs.

Undertake your career is like a young entrepreneur who will start an adventure and undertake a new business whose sustainability and success depend on his approach, skills, training, perceptions, and vision. Thus, a startup allows one to build experiences whose objective is to give rise to learning, which, in turn, will allow one to build a sustainable business. Similarly, for a global worker, the opportunities he seizes must allow him a fruitful learning that enriches his portfolio of experiences that must converge with his vision and develop his skills. Suppose the diploma obtained is formed by the different subjects and modules taught to the student or learner. In that case, the professional career is guided by vision and built by experience. Therefore, the worker would have the flexibility to manage his career in conditions of uncertainty and instability. This is how a "pivot mindset" would be put in place. From now on, nothing follows a linear trajectory, a scale that must be climbed step by step and whose next phase is programmed and predictable with precision and certainty. Everything changes and moves in all directions. You must know how to locate the flow you want to follow and be able to change direction at the time you deem most appropriate and suitable. As Jenny Blake said, pivoting takes the form of a circle, a loop, which calls upon movement and continuous learning. Nothing is acquired, and nothing is lost forever.

Nothing is linear, and everything is subject to constant change, which implies agility and insight.

Like a startup, the vital function of a successful and comprehensive professional career is learning. You have to learn constantly to progress and especially know when to persevere and when to pivot. The learning validated by the experience and the opportunities seized would allow us to reach a certain maturity and decide whether it is the right time to pivot or persevere. In this sense, we must be entrepreneurs to successfully manage our careers in liquid times where nothing is stable and permanent, to create added value, and to find our place in the global labor market. The most important thing at this level is to be aware of the importance and crucial role of learning that begins with education but finds its continuity in the experiences (internships, volunteering, etc.) that will validate it, strengthen it, and develop skills. Suppose the world is a global system where everything is connected and interdependent. In that case, we are interested in being not only global citizens but also global workers so as not to stop progressing and evolving. Everyone is the entrepreneur of their career.

It is about wearing the cap of sustainable entrepreneurship in construction, management, and professional career change. The latter consists of a lifestyle that every entrepreneur will claim. In this sense, the entrepreneur should be a leader and responsible for his decisions and the consequences that emanate from them; active and reactive, constantly learning and always looking for up-to-date information; pragmatic, take action and focus on the feasibility and concretization of new ideas and projects, and flexible in the sense that everything supports modification and change. That said, long-term thinking does not mean planning for well-defined, well-traced plans and strategies, but rather having an overview of the various factors and circumstances that may affect the pre-established strategies, and above all, to be able to update this great image as changes take place. Updating is possible if one is always open to learning, so one acquires more skills and knowledge and will no longer fear modifying a strategy or changing objectives. Sustainable entrepreneurship is now necessary in an unstable and uncertain time.

The integration of the labor market, the launch of a new career, or the integration of a labor market abroad are not so easy or obvious tasks. Like an entrepreneur, we would constantly ask ourselves questions, question the feasibility of our ideas and projects, and question the credibility and the updating of the information we have. This applies both to a fresh graduate and to the manager of a large company. The uncertain times in which our professional careers are built leave no one immune from surprises and unforeseen events. Just like an entrepreneur, you have to ask yourself:

- In what field do you want to develop a professional career?
- What skills do you need to have or develop to be successful in the field?

The answer to these two questions helps guide our thinking and make decisions that suit us, and that can be perceived by others as confusing or unexpected.

Referring to Amar BHIDE and drawing on her writings, I would say that to lead our career path, the following questions must be asked and answered:

1. What are my goals? ➔ Clarify your goals!
2. How can I reach them? ➔ Putting a strategy in place.
3. Am I able to implement the chosen approach?

1. Clarify your objectives: what are my objectives?

Our objectives determine, to a large extent, the size and scope of the professional career we want to build. This includes:

- Analyze the situation we find ourselves in: am I a fresh graduate with no experience or experienced in a particular field? Am I an expert in a field? Am I compatible with market demands? Does the labor market require the skills and know-how that I have? What kind of career do I want to build?
- Identify the assets you have that will help you achieve your objectives. For example, skills, networking, experience…
- Periodically ask if your objectives have changed or have been modified.

Therefore, clarifying the objectives requires an explicit reflection but also a reconciliation of what we want to achieve with what we are ready to sacrifice (time, money, old position, financial stability, migration, etc.) to point out very specific and precise objectives, which will determine the path to follow and the way to reach them. It would be interesting to look for recruiters who share the same objectives as ours and are looking for similar expertise and skills. Such an analysis makes it possible to adjust our objectives to the market and specify the shortcomings and the skills to be developed to achieve our objectives. Clarifying objectives requires a well-developed perception of the market and a fairly broad view and overview of the different current circumstances and the probable future, which can intervene in the adjustment of objectives. Having objectives is to be prepared to look to the future while taking into account the current state of affairs.

2. **Implementing a strategy**: how can I achieve my objectives?

Prioritize the opportunities and issues we will face. Distinguish between opportunities that will improve our skills and those that will limit us from getting money! Also, distinguish critical and serious problems that can hinder the development of our career or slow down the speed of achieving our objectives from those that are normal or essential for growth and the development of any career or new learning.

We must always find a way to be competitive in the labor market and expand our competitiveness. As we have always said, the one who does not move forward retreats. This requires the development of experiences, learning new skills, launching a new career, developing an innovative scope in one's field of activity, evolving from an employee to a coach, and then becoming a consultant.

Along the way in the development of the strategy and all along the steps to reach our objectives, we will face different challenges, take different risks, and be exposed to different alternatives or even contradictory pieces of advice. Once we have set our goals and how to achieve them, we will no longer be fragile and sensitive to ambiguity but rather comfortable with the instability of our environment.

3. Execution of the strategy: Can I implement and execute the chosen approach?

Great ideas do not guarantee outstanding or exceptional performance (Amar Bhide, 1996). This is why we must always examine ourselves, self-criticize and above all, always design-new paths that best correspond:

- To our profile, skills, experiences, training;
- To objectives that may change over time as a result of special circumstances

It is a question of the effectiveness of the resources. It means at our disposal, which allows us to implement the strategy and achieve the desired objectives. It is the question of whether the financial means at my disposal, training, experience, time, and current and future conditions of the market allow me to carry out the steps set? Should I call on an expert to guide me and clarify certain points or proceed independently?

As our careers develop or change, we need to be able to play new and different roles and put on multiple hats. A fresh graduate is not a manager, is not a coach, and is not a consultant.

An entrepreneur is concerned about the sustainability and continuity of his projects. So, he is interested in developing and improving his activities. This is possible when he is interested in real problems, by going back to the source and not rush events or looking for easy troubleshooting solutions whose efficiency is not optimal. By having a holistic vision, the entrepreneur would be able to adjust his strategy and reflections and distinguish the problems that must be solved by short-term solutions from those for whom background treatment is essential for the sustainability and prosperity of the project. Instead of continuing to post your curriculum vitae, focusing on developing and forming a program that brings value to your experience and training would be more interesting.

Instead of focusing on the amount of salary in the first place, you have to question the value of the experience you will have. Will the learning you will acquire allow you to progress and enrich your curriculum vitae and increase your market value?

Therefore, an entrepreneur is a combination of two qualities: perseverance and flexibility. He is not discouraged, despaired, or demoralized, getting stuck at the first failure, hindrance, or change. He assesses risks; he always tries to learn from his failures, point out shortcomings, and listen to the market and experts. Thus, an entrepreneur perseveres but does not rush into the wall either. He should be flexible and willing to change strategy, adapt products, and collaborate. This combination of perseverance and flexibility will open the door to a "pivotal state of mind."

The career plans we make and the projections are filled with uncertainty; even our personal life is based on unstable circumstances and elements. That is why we need to dose the piloting ingredients. This is how we will manage to steer a professional career in an uncertain and unstable environment.

The deepening of all knowledge requires experimentation. Thus, learning results from the opportunities captured to experiment, deepen and enrich a very specific knowledge. We must also be aware that we will not experiment with all knowledge at once but rather with knowledge in the same direction as our vision, which will facilitate the next step and the achievement of our next objective. In this sense, it is not a question of working hard but of working intelligently, of following one's vision and not scattering one's ambitions to move forward with the right step.

Therefore, there is no magic recipe for those who succeed in these conditions of extreme uncertainty. One must be aware of the unstable nature of modern times and succeed in being flexible so as not to be broken but rather pivot and change shape quickly and effectively whenever deemed necessary. In this sense, to progress and advance, we must:

- **Learn in a permanent and continuous way.**

We learn by playing, taking classes, having new experiences, taking new jobs, and changing countries of residence…We must always extract an added value, find pleasure in learning something new, be active, and not content ourselves with passive receptivity. Observe dynamically, self-assess to be able to position oneself in relation to the market and be aware of its current skills and specify the potential skills to be competitive and requested by the market in question. Learning is about analysis, criticism, reasoning and reflection, flexibility, and the ability to adopt change. Being open to learning means wanting to explore, appreciate mobility and develop flexibility.

- **Develop new skills**

The role of today's workers is no longer limited to knowledge; an engineer can acquire commercial skills. With new technologies, information has become accessible and available. The role of workers then extended to a relational dimension (Blake, 2016). We need to know and be able to collaborate, communicate, share information, be open to differences to improve performance, face challenges, and make the most appropriate decisions. Knowledge, experience, and information are essential, but skills are even more essential. They are the ones that will allow you to lead a team, build relationships, manage emergencies, modify a strategy, take risks, and make decisions. Of course, everything is relative in the sense that it would be interesting to develop the skills that intersect with our current vision, experience, and knowledge. What do you want to learn? How do you want to become an expert? What skill, once developed, will allow you to move in the desired direction?

It is a way to ensure the continuity of your career. Even more, as noted by the sociologist Castell (2010), the structure of the labor market is characterized by its duality, and two types of work have arisen, namely "self-programmable labor," that is self-employment in which decision-making autonomy is attributed to employees. This type of worker can retrain and adapt to new tasks, skills, processes, technologies, and sources of information.

The second structure is generic labor. At this level, employees only execute instructions and do not have much scope for decision-making. They are easily replaceable, and the company can relinquish their services once the mission is completed. They "coexist in the same circuits with machines and unskilled labor from all over the world" (Manuel Castells, 2000). Where do you stand, and where do you want to be in the near future? What skills and knowledge will you need to be able to move from one category to another or even alternate between the two depending on the need of the position, mission, and environment?

- **Develop your portfolio of experiences.**

When you manage to develop experiences, it is an indicator of activity, flexibility, willingness, learning, and insight. Enriching one's experience does not necessarily mean being recruited by a firm or occupying a position in another company. Even if the opportunity does not present itself, you need to stimulate the circumstances, use your creativity, and entrepreneurial skills, draw attention to yourself, and think about the activities that will build your reputation and "personal brand." Think about what you like, but especially where you can excel. This shows that the person in question is good at seizing opportunities but also knows very well how to prepare himself to be ready when the opportunity presents itself and not to be out of phase, that he is accustomed to change, and that he is not afraid of movement. In this sense, nothing is left to chance. In one way or another, everything is prepared in advance and little by little. We have to think big but also look closely at the "bridges" that will allow us to reduce the gap between what we are today and what we want to be in one, two, or three years. You have to develop an entrepreneurial spirit.

New positions, new responsibilities, and new tasks must be tried out. Indeed, spending a lot of time in the same roles and responsibilities can confuse development and obstruct growth.

You must realize that graduation is just one step because being content with one is like being stuck in the land of the living dead. It just allows you to achieve the success that will keep you alive, like passing a recruitment contest.

In an uncertain and unstable environment, we must not fear failure. We must fear not to see clearly or learn from this failure. This latter is a prerequisite for learning that allows you to test your strengths, connections, and skills. This allows us to identify failures, deficiencies, and gaps that must be addressed.

With his pragmatic character and a strong inclination for action, an entrepreneur does not limit his thoughts and reflections to the problems and obstacles in his strategies, decisions, and objectives. With a broad perception and holistic vision, he manages to reconcile risk and opportunities, problems and solutions. To succeed and maintain one's success, it is necessary to continually question the future and the extent of the path followed and undertaken. Steering one's career is to be, at the same time, a practical, and active thinker to conceive one's way and not be limited to undergoing changes.

> **Learn then move, explore, experiment and develop interpersonal skills. Do not fear the movement. It will save you from sedentary living. It is instability that gives rise to opportunities.**

4. Pivot Career

The traditional concept of a professional career does not support the ups and downs. It is about following a linear path, deciding on a career, and working along a predetermined path. There is no room for risk-taking or uncertainty. It is a vision that flees all fog, and above all, it is a fixed strategy that does not support modifications. This pivotal mindset allows us to rotate/ reorient our perspectives and perceptions; this is what will make our mental strength, which will be useful to us to meet the challenges and unforeseen events arising from the instability of our environment. For a pivot, what matters most is the following step, which is why they must be courageous and should not fear the unexpected, the unstable. They take responsibility because they have always been responsible for their learning. They fear redundancy and stability because he constantly looks for opportunities that only change brings. Like in basketball, the pivot refers to movement and motion; his role is to score baskets, and his skill and agility will allow him not to lose balls.

> The fable of the frog: placed in a pot progressively containing hot water, the frog tries to adapt its body to the increase in temperature, up to a certain degree where it was unable to jump out of the container and unable to handle the great heat. It was scalded up.
>
> **You should know how to jump on time otherwise it will be too late.**

When should we pivot? If there is no progression, you are not moving in the direction of your vision, you are only achieving short-term goals, you are stuck in a position or a relationship, your skills or experience are not recognized by the market, and you cannot see the end of the tunnel. These are all signs that it is time to change your strategy, think differently, use your skills, your training, and your experiences differently, improve in a different way, and take a different look at the various elements surrounding you. Pivot and not persevere so as not to have the frog syndrome.

If our environment changes develop and we do not follow these changes, we will be surpassed and overwhelmed by events and things that are foreign to us. So, pivoting is having flexibility and agility to move at the right time and above all, be in tune with a world in full motion. Otherwise, we will be lost, and we will not be able to follow the flow without drowning.

The pivot refers to the change of strategy and not of vision. The goal is the same, but the way to achieve it differs. Thus, Ries (2010) defines the pivot as "a structured course correction, designed to test and experiment new paths, new opportunities, test new ideas, new strategies, methods, and approaches." So, the pivot is not done on a whim, nor by chance, but rather in a methodical way. It is about getting ready for a new and relevant direction. Thus, the career pivot is "an intentional and methodical process that allows one to navigate with agility in career changes" (Jenny Backe, 2016). Pivoting our careers has become a new norm. The pivot prepares us for the next stage, and it is it that counts the most. It is a guarantee of continuity, development, progression, and updating.

The pivot is a key element to personalize your career. Circumstances change, connections change, and things develop; we will always be exposed to new challenges. What are we going to do? Will we get stuck, fit into the frame, or find another way? The pivot connects the different variables and is always interested in what is unstable; he does not settle for the acquired but always asks what is uncertain and unclear and what he can do if circumstances change in one way or another. He has a vision and is always looking for new alternatives and ways to achieve his goals.

5. How to Successfully Make a Change of Direction

No judgment
You have to get out of your box, be open to development

and change, broaden your perception, and have a global view of the market and its changes. This will help us avoid being prisoners of our own reality. By freeing ourselves from judgment, we will be more open to innovations and creations, we will design new paths to facilitate the progression of our career, and above all, this will allow us to get away from the bad decisions resulting from false conclusions. Non-judgment minimizes risk, broadens our range of alternatives, and adjusts us to change. The more we get rid of judgment, the more flexible and mobile we are.

Have a vision

The decision to pivot requires insight and an objective state of mind. We must not lose sight of our objective to know what path to take, to be prepared for the changes, and not have trouble changing our strategy.

Have connections

It is about the network of connections we have and have access to, whether direct or indirect. It is an actor, whether it is a friend, a neighbor, a colleague, an acquaintance, a friend of a friend, a supplier, a customer who brings you new ideas and different perceptions, who has a new insight, with whom you can discuss and whose discussion will enrich you and who can introduce you to a new network and expand yours.

Career portfolio

When you have identified your goals, values, and vision, you build your career and portfolio. At this level, it is no longer about experiences to demonstrate your skills but rather about your career, the positions you have held, or the diverse missions in the same position, which will highlight your achievements and your qualities. By having a vision, knowing ourselves, and being aware of our strengths, we will know what the market demands, its possible changes, and the required skills. Hence, there will no longer be room for the "whim;" everything will be reflected and prepared in advance. A homogeneous, rich, diversified, and above all, complementary career portfolio must be established. It must reflect a certain continuity between the different experiences.

A better self-knowledge

You have to be able to determine your values and strengths and be aware of the income a specific position can bring. You must know how to explore and determine the most important values the person in question wishes to have. Exploring values and objectives is based on self-assessment and self-criticism, reflecting on what we do. Whether it fits our skills and preferences, it allows us to move forward, and whether it meets our ambitions and vision. Therefore, we will start collecting the clues, identify the strengths and be aware of the gaps so that we can take a holistic view of the environment, the market, and our position in that big picture. We will learn to see far and blurry without fearing this uncertainty because it is part of the dynamics of modern times.

Thus, it is in this sense that, like society, the pivot of a career is a matrix composed of different variables that interact to set up, reproduce and change a professional career.

Think In Terms Of Alternatives

"As long as we are executing the plan well, hard work yields results."
— Eric Ries

Generally, the major concern of students is graduation. They pass the academic year and move from one year to the next until graduation. They studied well and prepared for the exams, and it was done; they passed. Thus, the problem of academic failure is solved. But, will this allow the student to evolve, move forward, get a job systematically, compete with candidates, and succeed in his job interview? I do not think so! Studying well allows you to succeed and get the diploma; no more. That is why you have to think big. To have the eagle's vision, this piercing look endowed with terrible precision allows the eagle to aim at its prey in a hectic environment.

Similarly, you must have a clear vision to look ahead into the future. This is how you will undertake the right actions and the right reflections to achieve the goal set in advance. Take a step back, and observe your environment and the position you occupy. Provide an overview, "a helicopter view," to detect the different alternatives and achieve the set objective.

Thinking is a cognitive activity that we use at different stages of our lives: to choose the faculty to enter, decide the future of a romantic relationship, change our career, get out of a financial problem, choose the color of the car to buy…before we make a decision or go one way or the other, we think, but do we all think the same way? Is the reflection stable in time? I seriously doubt it.

We have heard a lot about how we cannot educate our children with the same approach as our parents and our grandparents, that the children of today are not the children of yesterday and will not be the same as the children of tomorrow. Have you wondered why? Because society changes, people change their mentality, state of mind, and perceptions. This is mainly due to the development of technology and digitalization, which have accelerated the pace of change and promoted the instantaneous nature of information. Hence the importance of reflection: we must be able to reflect.

We have to pay attention to a very important detail! When we talk about reflection, it does not mean that we will limit ourselves to solving a problem or simply making the best choice among different alternatives, but rather to move forward, develop, improve, and ensure constructive continuity.

The practical purpose of reflection is to enable us to understand what is happening around us, react appropriately, and change the course of events in our favor. After all, our brain is not just a store of experiences, knowledge, and information. To think in a practical and useful way is to understand what is going around us, or to understand a particular situation and then to know how to act adequately to the situation in question and if necessary, change the course of things to our benefit and take advantage of it. Therefore, reflection implies activity and excludes all passivity. When we learn to think effectively, we become the master of our own destiny. Understanding is not an end in itself but rather the first step. If we understand, it is to act afterward, to take appropriate action in a given situation.

Flexibility excludes rigidity. Nothing is rigid or permanent, as in the information age and in times of uncertainty. Flexibility allows one to face challenges, seize and adapt to new opportunities, embrace change, create one's own flow, and not get lost. In this sense, reflection makes it possible to change the course of things to our advantage, allowing us to pivot and always remain mobile and flexible.

On the other hand, do not be afraid of thinking differently. Do not let the fear of uncertainty, change, judgment, and criticism inhibit your thinking, imagination, and visualization. Trust yourself, believe in your dreams, be aware of your potential and be open to difference. Reflection has the same effect as sports on our body; the more we practice, the more we strengthen our muscles, improve our endurance, will be prepared to practice more difficult exercises, and above all, get used to and enjoy making more physical effort.

Thinking big allows seeing new opportunities, opening new horizons, taking risks, and moving forward. We are not looking for easy answers or safety but rather for new opportunities and learning to add value to everything we do, improve, and develop ourselves.

Thinking big requires continuous learning. There is always something new to learn, discover, and know. Explore new paths, discover new territories, learn new skills, expand your knowledge, and create new connections.

1. Have a Helicopter View

Imagine you are in a maze that you want to get out of. You are at the front door. What you are going to do is look at the different paths and choose the one that seems right to you. If the path does not turn out to be the right one, you will choose another; each time, you will explore and experience the different possible routes and alternatives until you find the right path for the exit. At this level, we do not have complete information. All we know is the entrance of the path; as for the rest, we have no idea. We have to try to find out. We do not know where each road leads, at what level it is cut off, and which road is connected with which other road. We will therefore proceed with logical reasoning based on the information available. We do not have a broad perception to think in broad terms.

Now imagine you are equipped with a drone connected to your smartphone, which will allow you to have a general overview of the maze and, therefore, to select the paths that lead to the exit, the connections between the different routes, to try one of them and get out of the maze. At this level, perception is very broad, the image is larger, and the information we have on this maze is complete.

Without a drone, the logic used to choose the way out is consistent with limited perception, which may result in an inappropriate or false action. With the drone, it is different as we have a broad perception, so we will perceive things differently and therefore have a completely different approach.

A broad perception allows one to have as much information as possible and subsequently to make logical choices according to this information. Thus, limited perception leads to limited logic. Perception is very important because it determines logic, large image, and creativity. If we want to think in broad and general terms and to think big, we have to develop our perception. It provides the raw material that logic will handle later. Thus, a broad perception allows one to have more information and see bigger and, therefore, have a more developed logic.

When faced with a problem to solve, it would be interesting to take a broad look, to have a general view of the subject so as not to be trapped and stuck in details. So, firstly we will detect the possible alternatives and take advantage of more flexibility. Secondly, we will be able to evaluate the various alternatives. Then, we will refine and narrow this broad reflection into a more specific, detailed, and focused reflection to end with a precise reflection. To think big is to visualize both the end of the tunnel and the big image, or even to preview the objectives and the territory, which will allow us to think in terms of alternatives, see the possible paths, and therefore be open to learning, be optimistic, consistent and strongly determined.

Thinking in broad terms allows us not to focus on every detail and thus not to distract our attention, not to be motionless at the first unforeseen event but rather to give ourselves flexibility that narrow-minded people cannot have. This elasticity arises from the ability to move from broad concepts to more precise ones and vice versa. To think wide is not to think in disorder; it is about looking at things from different perspectives, getting interested in others' points of view, and not being limited to one's reality. We have to put ourselves in others' shoes and think about one subject taking into consideration the other's history, experience, and concerns. To put oneself in the place of the other, one must see beyond oneself, personal interests, and experiences. You have to develop your curiosity, get out of your box and discover that of the others.

Thus, it is not a matter of fearing ambiguity because we know perfectly well that the "helicopter view" is not entirely clear but allows us to have an overview. This overall view will guide our efforts. As we progress along our paths, we develop and enrich our experiences, knowledge, and information, allowing us to get to the bottom of things, go to the details and end with more elaborate reflections.

This is only possible when we are connected to the world around us when we are a part of it as a whole and perceive it as a matrix with different components. In this way, we would be able to take a fairly broad view that includes different variants that allow our reasoning to be related to the reality of things and to foresee, as far as possible, the various changes and above all, not to lose our grip in the face of unforeseen events and uncertainties.

2. Develop Our Perceptions

Our skills, knowledge, different learning, reactions, behaviors, and responses are the part that is apparent and visible to everyone, but what led us to take this or that path, to proceed in a very special way, to change direction? This is the invisible part of the iceberg; these are our perceptions. The perceptions we build and develop of different circumstances, changes that take place, and unforeseen events that are necessary affect our choices and orientations to a large extent. On the other hand, there are situations where resolution takes time and issues that we need to learn to live with, such as COVID. In fact, it would be wiser to develop our perception to better manage the situation than to stay stuck and unable to move forward in life. Hence, the interest is raised in perception in that it makes it possible to change the angle of vision to perceive new horizons and take new directions.

a. It All Starts with Perception

Nowadays, the real change is to perceive information differently to create added value, impose oneself, and carve out a place for oneself. Being in liquid and uncertain times implies constant movement, change, and increased demand for agility. But to move, it is necessary to determine the direction to take, which is not very obvious if we have to change our perspectives each time: change careers, manage relationships, or launch a new project. In this sense, perception is an indispensable tool if we want to swim in unstable currents of water without being carried away or swamped by the flows, but rather in the desired direction. Moreover, a large part of the errors of thought we make are, at the base, errors of perception. A job with an attractive salary is not necessarily an opportunity to develop our professional careers. Sometimes it is blocking, isn't it?

Furthermore, our environment is full of events, situations, stimuli of all kinds, unforeseen events, and changes that we perceive and react to accordingly. As we grow and evolve, throughout our education, from kindergarten to university, knowledge and information are passed on to us, whether it is about beliefs, culture, or life simply. From there, the brain begins to make some sense of the information that reaches it, it is perception, and it is this sense that will determine our view of the world around us. Thus, perception is the meaning we give to the information, situation, events, and people we are exposed to. Therefore, perception is the starting point for our reflection; it is a matter of perceiving the labor market situation, processing the information, and then triggering a process of reflection.

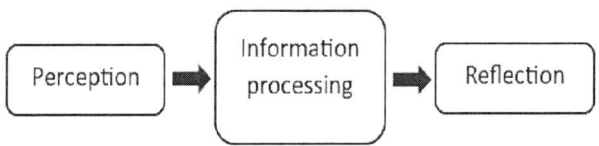

To determine the actions to be taken, we tend to rely on certainty, real facts, and truths because they give us feelings of security and comfort. As a result, we find ourselves stuck in a routine, in what is outdated, while the world changes and evolves. We opt for actions that slow down the change to defend the knowledge and skills acquired. Thus, it would be difficult to persuade someone to change their behavior (quit smoking, take risks, etc.) in a logical way but rather by linking action to feeling, something that perception excels at making a reality. Perception largely determines the effectiveness of the logic followed in our reflection. Indeed, logic derives its meaning from perception. Suppose you are able to explore a person's perception. In that case, you can understand or even predict their logic, feelings, and behavior. A logic based on misperception leads to inappropriate responses and reactions.

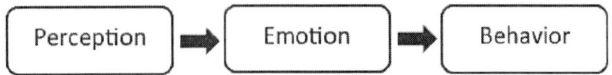

However, this is impossible in liquid times, where uncertainty is the only certain truth, changes occur at high speed, and agility is no longer an option. Flexibility is the best quality for adapting, evolving, and learning continuously. Thus, if our perceptions are not appropriate, so will our actions. Being a good driver does not mean you will take the best path, just as being excellent at studying does not mean having an unfailing professional career. To achieve this, you need to continuously scan the market, be open to diversity and have a flexible state of mind.

Perception is the ability to see the situation from different angles and bring different readings to the circumstances that arise. In this sense, perception is an open, generative system giving rise to possibilities and alternatives, allowing us to manage the instability and diversity of the world around us and in which we evolve and develop while remaining focused on our goals. It is thanks to the generosity of alternatives that flexibility takes place.

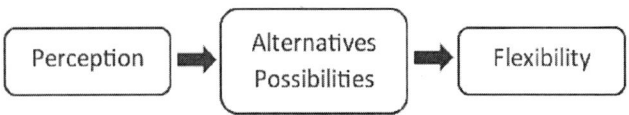

Technology Has Changed Our perceptions and Our Emotions

You are looking for a job, and you come across an offer whose job description and the type of contract proposed correspond to your skills. You see it as an opportunity, and while you are anxious about getting a job, you feel encouraged, relieved, and positive. So you are going to apply and be optimistic. It is in this sense that your emotions follow your perceptions. Any change in perception will therefore lead to a change in emotions. Once the perception triggers an emotion, the latter will lead and guide the action. Indeed, in our daily lives, for example, to find the way to school, prepare for an interview, cross the road, decide to enter into a romantic relationship, or accept a job. We start from the perceptions we continuously form. If your perception is correct, your answer will be correct. Otherwise, if your perception is inadequate, your answer will not be right, even if you have infallible logic.

Positiveness, joy, and inner peace are not the result of certain situations but rather a way of seeing things. Positive thoughts are a form of assertion to which your feelings will adapt. What you think affects your feelings. Think about what can make you happy and positively perceive the world around you, the circumstances, and the changes.

It is not a matter of deciding whether the glass is half-full or half-empty. It is important to see it as both half-empty and half-full so we appreciate what we have and look for the possibilities to fill the other half and decide what to do to reach the desired level. It is a matter of conscience, responsibility, and perception. So, thinking about happiness and success and visualizing your ambitions allows you to generate ideas and possibilities and then try to set them up to finally evaluate them and see if you have made the right choice and taken the right path or have to explore other possibilities and paths. Moreover, enjoying good health concerns both the body and the brain. Having an active body means exercising, moving, dancing, and filling the space with our body movements. It is to provide physical effort while meeting challenges. It is having a certain discipline. That said, making a physical effort allows you to get rid of extra calories and regain your energy, fitness, and healthy look, breathe better, and go on your way with a new breath. Like physical activity, mental activity keeps you always awake, caring, and keeping pace with the changing world around us. Being mentally active is learning continuously. In our world, there are many learning sources, not just academic studies or reading. We can learn a new cuisine, language, know-how, and skills. That is how we will be able to dig in ourselves, meet the challenges, continue to evolve, and pursue the process, and as it is often said, those who do not progress recede.

However, we must pay attention to a very important point: do not prefer safe and certain paths, do not get stuck in what is acquired and predictable; be in free movement; focus on the "process" rather than the result and have confidence in yourself and in your perception. Perceive differently and create your own flow.

b. The Gap Between Perception and Reality

Do you know the story of the six wise men who are all blind and who tried to describe an elephant? This is the best example to give to describe the gap that may exist between perception and reality. Each of them touches the elephant and describes it to the others. The first touches the elephant's ear and describes it as a thick cover. The second touches the tusk and says that the elephant is pointy and sharp. The third puts his hand on one of the elephant's legs and finds it looks more like a tree trunk. The fourth grabs the tail and claims the elephant looks more like a rope. Feeling the elephant's side with his hand, the fifth describes it as a wall. The sixth, after touching the head, describes it as a rock.

Who is right, and who is wrong? Each of them is right, from his own perspective, from his point of view. They do not have a complete picture of the elephant. Each of them presents a very limited perception of the elephant; in this sense, the perception of each represents his own reality.

Our reality is our perception at a given moment.

The famous phrase of the founder of general semantics, Alfred Korzibsky, "The map is not the territory," which we often hear, evokes the gap between perception and reality. At a given moment, the perception of each of us is only one's own reality. Indeed, all that the human brain does is build realities. It receives information through the different sensory organs and builds a reality. Thus, the human brain is no longer the mirror that projects reality as such. But rather, it builds the reality of each of us, which emanates from our own perspectives. Therefore, by the map, we designate the perception at a given moment, and by the territory, we designate the reality. So, a change in perception leads to a change in reality, and our life will change afterward. What we perceive is our own reality at some point. Throughout our lives, we face different challenges, trials, and difficulties to overcome but also opportunities to seize, new paths to conquer, and new horizons to explore, which will shape and determine our perceptions and realities at every moment of our lives. It is a question of perception at a given moment and not reality. So, when we change maps, we change territories, and when we change perceptions, we change reality. For example, our perception of time at the age of 20 differs from that at the age of 40. When we are young, we have the impression that we have a lot of time to learn, achieve our goals, and enjoy life. We even have the impression that the time is long and does not go by quickly enough. We hear from the young and the less young who want to grow up and are eager to start their working lives. At 40 years of age, or even before that, we see things differently. Time goes by so quickly that we do not realize it. One must take advantage of every moment of one's life to learn to develop and to go forward. A first perception will lead to another. After that, the realities of each of us change. Those who once saw education as a source of fatigue now see it as a means of development and improvement. Those who found the time long now feel that it is going at high speed.

Reality is essentially based on two important elements: context and past experiences. This determines the realities built by our brains and our perceptions. The perception of a situation or something largely depends on its context. A change of context leads to a change of perception. The day you lose one of your parents, you will know nothing will be the same. You will have a new reality that will derive from a new perception, which, in turn, will emanate from a new context. If something is perceived as good, it is because it is in an appropriate context. Thus, with the presence of context, our brain builds a reality that will not be the same in the absence or presence of a different context. In the context, our brain builds its own reality and its current perception that is different from reality. The context consists of the environment, the set of circumstances in which we form our realities, and our perceptions at a given time. Let's take De Bono's great example: When you are hungry and given a slice of cheese, you perceive it as food and a meal to satisfy your hunger. However, when you sit down with friends for a drink after work and are presented with the same bit of cheese, you perceive it as an aperitif. When you change the context, you change the perception and reality.

On the other hand, our direct and indirect experiences with the world around us influence, shape, and reformulate our realities. Indirect experiences come from the knowledge and lessons transmitted to us by our parents, teachers, culture, society, family, friends and colleagues, neighbors, school, and university. They teach us what they have discovered and what they have learned. They teach us their experiences.

Direct experiences represent our personal experiences built from our adventures and misadventures, successes and failures, challenges, explorations, and discoveries. That is what makes us who we are. All these direct and indirect experiences are classified in boxes in our brains. Suppose something does not fit into one of those boxes. In that case, it is considered bad, inappropriate, risky, dangerous, and therefore we no longer feel safe. Thus, our brain is arranged in boxes in which the definitions of the different objects and situations, the classification of the different things, and the profiles of people are stored. The formulation of these boxes is based on our direct and indirect experiences. These boxes represent principles and limits that have been the subject of society and community conventions. In this sense, if we live in boxes, it is because it is simpler, more reassuring, and more secure. We tend to eliminate anything that does not fit our boxes, experiences, and principles. However, this fits perfectly only with a closed, stable, and frozen environment, which does not change or develop. We live in a world that is continually changing. Perceptions are changing and evolving, and emotions and behaviors are changing too. What was not accepted yesterday can be tolerated in the future. Do not just think "inside the box." Step out of your bubble; free your boundaries; push them; and give yourself the opportunity to see far, wide, and differently; think, ask yourself questions, and fall and rise. To keep up with the world, we must be flexible, courageous, bold, open, and curious.

Thus, each person has their own perspectives, memories, and experiences; therefore, their own perceptions and reality, a reality not necessarily that of everyone.

Awareness of this gap allows us to master and control our judgments, feelings, and behavior. We will learn to accept others and be flexible, not to rush into excusing or blaming someone or to get into decision-making, but to take a step back, take a breath, see the background, and act.

Over time, things, the environment, and conditions change. Suppose they are not accompanied by a change in perception. In that case, the gap will widen, and a distortion will take place between perception and reality. This can lead to problems of communication and problems of integration in professional, social, and even personal life.

c. The Logic of Perception

"You do not believe what you see; you see what you already believe," said Wayne Dyer. We live in a matrix of different axes, economic and social environments….and each person lives in their own bubble, representing only the reality and perception of each of us. How we perceive things determines the logic of information processing, which determines our actions. Each person has their own logic bubble that derives from their own perceptions. In this sense, we are all heroes of our own stories. That is why, in a conflict, both parties can be right. Everyone is right according to his own perception and his own logic bubble.

The logic bubble is the set of perceptions of different circumstances, knowing that perception is formed in layers. One perception leads to another, leading to other perceptions. This set of superposed layers of perceptions puts in place a well-determined logic, the bubble of the logic of each of us, to process the information released from our perceptions, such as observations and possibilities, which subsequently lead to actions. These actions will allow others to know what we really want, discover our thoughts, understand us, and know our beliefs and feelings. These actions speak volumes about our image of ourselves and who we are.

Thus, each person acts perfectly logically according to their logic bubble. Therefore, what is limited is perception and not logic. Logic is correct for a very limited perception. If we broaden our perceptions, think bigger, and are not content with just seeing further than the tip of our nose, we will see wider, and therefore, the logic will change. Thus, if the perception is limited, the logic will be correct, but the resulting action will be inappropriate. This will affect our communications with others because by putting in place improper actions, we will be misunderstood, and our actions will not be perceived in the desired way.

> **Limited perception + correct logic ➔ inappropriate action**

The human brain forms its perceptions by choosing to see the world from its own perspective, to see it in a particular way that differs from one person to another. Human perception allows us to take an even broader view and consider the various alternatives that may exist. As a result of a limited perception at a given point in time, a choice is made that is quite logical but is perfectly consistent with the limited perception. In other words, if we do not have all the information, we will make a logical choice based on the information we have. We cannot build it if we do not perceive all the pieces that make up the puzzle. So, the more the perception is developed and broad, the more it allows us to see, think bigger, have more information and possibilities, and detect more opportunities. Indeed, the most ordinary tasks, like creativity, occur at the perception level. By seeing bigger, we develop new perceptions and logic, giving birth to creativity. While routine tasks are tasks conditioned by very particular circumstances; hence, the absence of logic, choice, and, therefore, the absence of reflection. It is a perception that repeats itself but does not develop.

Perception always seeks to give meaning to objects, situations, and the world. It gives meaning to that what is present.

d. Strengthening Our Perceptions

Thought and perception are characterized by their interdependence, with one affecting the other. Developing perception makes it possible to have better reasoning and avoid making bad decisions. However, how can we strengthen our perceptions? In the following, we will present points from De Bono's work to improve perceptive thinking.

1. Get your head out of the water: avoid sinking into failures, mistakes, and flaws. Instead of opting for a problem-solving attitude, opt for development, construction, and improvement. Do not let yourself be poisoned by negative points and failures. On the contrary, focus on opportunities for improvement and on your potential.
2. "The goal is nothing; the movement is everything." No judgment blocks you in a binary situation, accept or reject, tolerate or contest, love or hate. Judgment can only be useful in a stable world. However, every day, we experience changes of all kinds, which will lead to a change of perceptions and thus, a movement in our ideas and the links between concepts and ideas; it is the flexibility of the mind. If, in the past, the employer had to look for qualified people with skills

to hire them, now it is up to the candidate to highlight his skills, make himself stand out, and appear on professional networks such as LinkedIn to get hired. Things change, and the world and perceptions change; we must opt for movement.

3 To think of an alternative is not to engage in utopia. Instead of seeking the conclusion to be drawn from this or that situation as quickly as possible, it would be more interesting to consider the various possibilities. It is interesting to always keep in mind different alternatives for two reasons:

➢ The first possibility does not mean it is the best, so there is always room for improvement.
➢ Thinking in terms of alternatives allows us to compare, evaluate and ultimately choose the best options.

Therefore, you must always keep in mind the different possibilities to use them when necessary. Instead of being stuck in the face of an unexpected or unforeseeable change, you will know how to act and which direction to take.

> **Change in thinking results from changes in perceptions**

e. The Importance of Perceptive Acuity

The pressure we experience every day in work, family commitments, and professional relationships, the immersion in the strategies developed to achieve our objectives, the time constraint, and the speed of change that must be faced and managed at every stage of our lives, all this narrows our thoughts, lowers our attitudes, limits our perceptions and leaves us frozen in a specific area. For some, it is the comfort zone; for others, it is the routine. But from the moment you begin to ask yourself questions, question your judgments, compare your perceptions, and ask yourself what is the development of your own reality, the end of the path you are taking, the possibilities that may be offered along the way, but also the problems and defects that may appear in the meanwhile. That is when you will start looking at your perceptive acuity, trying to develop it and making it sharper and more elaborate. Just like the eagle that scans the territory and targets its prey from above, it is about getting out of one's bubble and bringing an external look at the situation in which you find yourself.

Perceptive acuity is our fog light allowing us to see through uncertainty, our lighthouse to clear the darkness of the path and predict the turning points ahead. The crystal ball of every fresh graduate, investor, and entrepreneur allows him to see beyond borders. It makes it possible to become more familiar with the environment's dynamic nature, be ahead in decision-making, and detect events, changes, anomalies, and opportunities that may take place and impact our strategy. It is a matter of taking into account all the signals, regardless of the intensity of their flow. Whether weak, medium, or strong, we must always integrate them into our perception.

We are in liquid times where everything changes and moves; nothing supports the static state. The winner is the first to have the information and make the decision that seems risky for others. This allows him to gain momentum and be ahead of the curve. It is all about time and speed. Indeed, the more you develop your perceptive acuity, the more open you will be to new ideas, events, trends, and opportunities. And you will be able to change your position to have different angles of view, point out the crucial element, and think about the different alternatives that make development possible. This is how perceptive acuity makes it possible to detect changes, prepare for, and even create uncertainties and unforeseen events.

HOW CAN WE KNOW THAT OUR PERCEPTIVE ACUITY IS BEING DEVELOPED?

- Be comfortable asking questions: why did this happen? What is it? What can happen in the near future? How did what happened impact what we are currently experiencing?
- Do not fear the change of position or opinion.
- Being able to detect the seed and ITS catalyst: the seed that every person carries in themselves; it is the skills they have, the degree they master, or the expertise they command. A seed only blooms and gives fruit if it is well cultivated. If not, it will be in a state of deep sleep until a catalyst detects its potential and exploits it to launch itself and succeed on the market.

f. The Duality: Seed-Catalyst

To acquire a perceptive acuity is to be able to detect your seed as well as the catalyst that will invest in the germination of your seed. Each of us has one or more seeds, which will have to be fed, cared for, and cultivated to give fruit. However, developing potential is a very important point. But the most important is the catalyst that will detect this potential, believe in the performance and profitability of your seed, and especially believe in your ability to adapt, develop and manage change and accelerate success. Identifying the catalyst for significant change allows us to shape our ideas, view future results, and prepare for uncertainty.

The catalyst can be:

- A person with sufficient perceptual acuity can harness strengths, reconceptualize what has already been done, and innovate to match your potential to current and future market demands. Catalysts challenge their perceptions and do not miss the opportunity to compare them with those of others on social networks, in events, and in meetings, reflect on their opinions to be aware of the diversity that may exist, put in mind the different possible hypotheses, visualize the new paths that can be offered and remain enthusiastic at the idea of the infinite opportunities. Catalysts are risk takers; they rely on facts for the detection of potentials but also on their imagination to take advantage of them and implement a new approach.

Your degree and skills are the seeds you must constantly maintain so that the day a catalyst comes along, you are in shape to take the lead and prosper.

- Events, new technology, and competitions are all catalysts that capture seeds and accelerate their growth. A seed can remain pending for a long time until a catalyst detects it, believes in it, and does something to make it flourish.

The idea is to develop your perceptive acuity to a degree where you will be the first catalyst of your seed. Ask yourself questions, be honest with yourself, and above all, determine the various interferences that block the way. Detect your potential.

Try to answer these questions:

1. How can you excel?
2. What is complementary to your training and/or work experience?
3. What are the market demands?
4. Do your skills match the market demands?

If the answer is No or Yes BUT:

- What is the gap?
- How can you narrow this gap?
- How can I compete with what exists?

If the answer is YES:

- What is my value creation?
5. How can I mark future employees?
6. How will I enter the job market?
7. What are the current and future changes?

8   What accelerated these changes?
9   What are the consequences of these changes?
10 Where can I find the catalysts that will grow my seed? In other words, what are the events, the communities, and the networks to integrate?

Of course, to answer all these questions, you have to be imaginative, not worry about projecting yourself into the future, be ready to make efforts, learn, and above all, face reality, and do not put yourself on the defense just to deny the change. The sharper your perceptive acuity, the more you will be able to identify catalysts and therefore perceive opportunities.

Think In Terms Of Opportunities

"You are a part of the symphony of the universe; you may be a listener or a musician."
— *Shams Tabrizi*

Life does not follow a linear trajectory, as does our career and opportunities along the way. Nothing is permanent or certain, and the unexpected occupies a large space in our daily lives. Opportunities are always linked to two elements:

Practice: what we undertake, practice, experiment.

Knowledge: what we know.

When opportunities present themselves, they do not consider our plans, forecasts, and circumstances. They show up without permission or warning. Sometimes they appear when you least expect them; they force you to decide to seize or miss them and make a decision within tight time limits. Sometimes we cannot detect them, which is why some people find themselves stuck in a position and have trouble progressing or evolving. It is because they do not know what opportunity to seize and in what opportunity to invest.

So, when you are ahead of time, you have time to analyze and do more research on the opportunity and prepare for it. Otherwise, we must dare to jump at the opportunity; in the good sense of the word, take the decision, and assume the risks it may entail.

1. Visualize the Opportunity

One should be aware that opportunity does not always take the form of something positive such as passing a competition, getting promoted, or getting a job. Sometimes failure in a recruitment competition is an opportunity in itself, the same for the dismissal or the fact of giving up one's career after the relocation of one's spouse, which is my case! You have to acquire the emotional strength to deal with the negative side and not be stuck and helpless in the face of new circumstances, but to take a fresh look and move forward. When an opportunity arises, try to seize it even if you do not fully master certain aspects and learn afterward. There is no hierarchy to follow strictly nor a linear trajectory to trace. Anything can take a turn at any time in our lives. One must prepare one's mind for the instability of circumstances and the uncertainty of times. Therefore, when an opportunity arises, you will know how to proceed and how to learn in a limited time. An opportunity does not wait for you; it puts pressure on you, and it is up to you to react.

a. Uncertainties-Opportunities-Mobility

Analytical tools play a relevant role in anticipating and accurately estimating the steps to be taken and determining the objectives and actions to be implemented. They play a key role in determining a linear strategic direction and a clear vision. This applies both to the company and to career management. However, with the development of the algorithm and in particular, with the new technology, the interdependence and interconnectivity of the world have increased, and stability, certainty, and uncertainty have taken on new dimensions and turning points. The question arises: is this enough in an uncertain liquid environment? Alternatively, do we need to integrate agility into developing our strategies and implementing action plans?

Indeed, the people who manage to make decisions in the most critical situations or in conditions of extreme ambiguity have put in place a flexible strategy and can perceive the opportunity in a crisis situation. They are endowed with a mindset to identify opportunities in uncertainty. Thus, the opportunity is the perception of uncertainty and the choice of actions to achieve the set objectives.

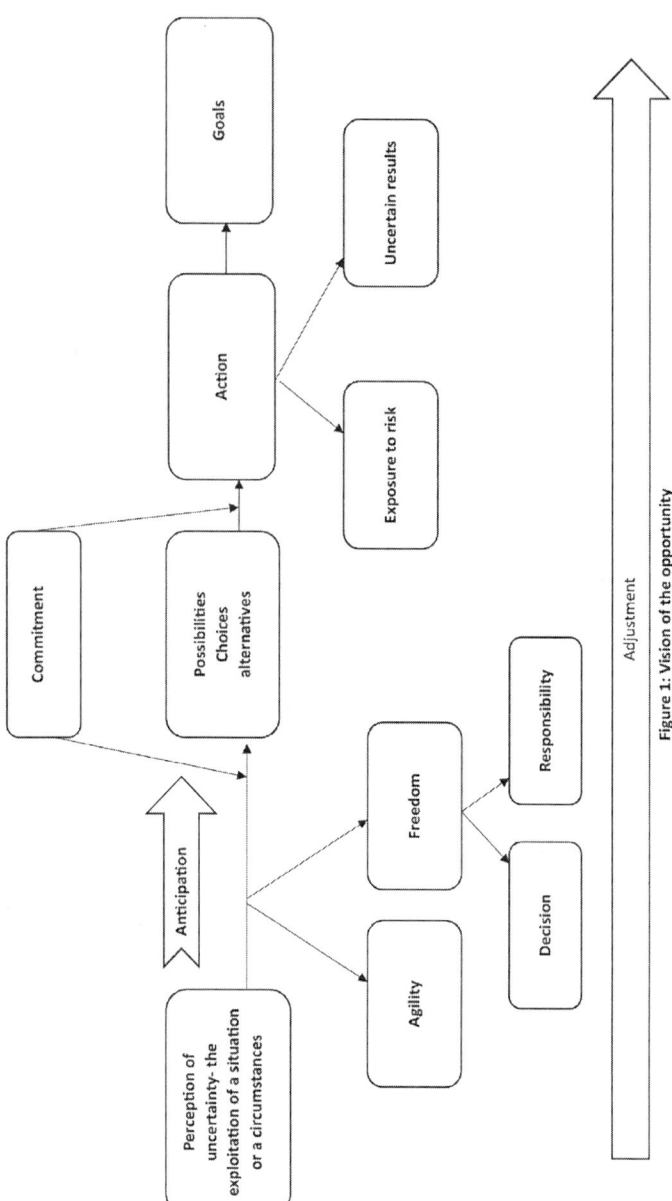

Figure 1: Vision of the opportunity

Uncertainty is not something to fear but rather to embrace. The source of this uncertainty and change must be clearly located, and the path to be taken must be identified. So, by diving in, you can discover possibilities and create value. In the uncertainty lies the possibilities that you can combine and arrange to create something new, different, topical, and especially valuable. The more you/ incorporate uncertainty into your considerations, the more your confidence will be developed, and you will be prepared to take new turns. It is about leading and managing uncertainty to find opportunities.

The perception of uncertainty is the ability to perceive a situation or circumstance as favorable or unfavorable to give rise to new alternatives and choices, open new horizons, and then decide on the necessary actions to transform these possibilities into changes, into reality, and make the necessary adjustments along the way. In this sense, action is the key factor of opportunity. It is the one who will make the possibilities come true and make the perception pragmatic. When we have a vision of the path to be taken and the objectives to be achieved, we can use our perception to generate alternatives, take advantage of the crisis situation and prosper under the right circumstances. According to our perception, we are interested in detecting the missing piece that others have not been able to identify or have done differently from what is currently being proposed. Hence, perception is very subjective; it is up to you to make this cognitive effort and observation to determine the opportunity that corresponds to you, your skills, your experiences, your training, and your profile. It is up to you to perceive the changes, information, crisis, the event and to come up with options. This step is not so obvious. To succeed, you must be:

Free: we must free ourselves from judgments, beliefs, restrictions, fears, and frustrations that limit our perceptions and goals and do not let us go far. We must be free to perceive differently and to make decisions that do not conform to standards. This does not mean giving up one's culture and beliefs but rather being open to differences and accepting change to be better and improve the current state of affairs. Freedom, therefore, implies the ability to make decisions and responsibility. Responsibility in the sense that each person is responsible for their choices, thoughts, actions, and commitments; nothing supports victimization. Being free to make the decision that fits your vision and be responsible for the consequences. Decision-making involves the ability to make a choice; it is being free to make the decision that corresponds to our vision and assume the consequences. When we make our choices, we become responsible for our decisions.

Agile: as we have explained earlier, agility requires mobility and flexibility. We must be open to any modifications or changes and act on time, not to be surprised by the unexpected but to accept them more and be reactive. Time is as important as mobility and flexibility.

Committed: the perception and the generating of possibilities and alternatives, the transition to action, and the implementation of a strategy require the commitment of the resources available and above all, the recognition of their limits and extent. The time needed for observation, learning, and research, the effort made, the financial means to finance training, and the availability of information are all resources to be committed to research, creating, and identifying opportunities.

After bringing one's own perception to try to generate opportunities, it is time to move to action and think about the actions to be taken and the steps to be followed to achieve one's goals. At this level, we must be aware that zero risk does not exist. There will always be risks to which you will be exposed. If you fail to communicate to your audience, if the product requires improvement; if economic and /or health conditions have changed in the meantime; if a new competitor appears; if the country's political conditions have deteriorated; if there are strikes, demonstrations, an increase in demand for your product. Therefore, the results are not certain. That said, this uncertainty may be favorable or unfavorable. You just have to prepare to not be in a state of surprise so you will take the necessary steps to manage your strategy and achieve your objectives.

In life, nothing is ever acquired; you have to be mobile, flexible, and endowed with a piercing perception to go ahead. Getting stuck in front of your computer, being satisfied by sending in your resume, and waiting for a recruiter to call you for the State to create positions is not the best approach. The passivity of waiting and immobility has never been the motto or path taken by successful individuals. Indeed, opportunity implies mobility, and the people who succeed embrace challenges, are not afraid of movement and change, and do not fear fog or blurred vision. In an uncertain world, one must be able to update one's environmental readings every time an event occurs, whether a structure changes or a problem occurs. If nothing is stable, our reading, vision, and perception of things should be as such.

b. Complementarity Between Problem-Opportunity and Solution-Profit

Opportunity is taking advantage of an unfavorable circumstance or exploiting a favorable situation. The question is, what is the difference between problem and opportunity?

On the one hand, just like a manager, in the presence of a problem, we must have the capacity to manage effectively, seek solutions and eliminate risks. It is a matter of securing the situation and stabilizing it to continue working. His role is to maintain the balance and progress of the work, but sometimes this maintenance implies the need for growth. However, the ability to solve problems allows you to get back on track; once the problem is solved, the right direction will be resumed.

In this sense, it is no longer a question of development and growth but rather of stability. When setting up a strategy, the manager will always face problems that he must solve and especially emergencies that must be addressed within time and space limits. However, not taking risks is ruling out opportunities, right? What do continuity and development entail once this is done and the problem is solved?

On the other hand, just like an entrepreneur, thinking in terms of opportunities is seeking the benefits and advantages that can be derived from a particular situation but also being ready to work more, increase the volume of effort and face more risks and more importantly, challenges. With the opportunity, we do not know exactly the direction to take and the different turns we may encounter. It is about accepting and managing ambiguity while being flexible to adjust our strategy in the process and achieve our objectives.

Should we think of a solution or an opportunity?

We are in liquid times where nothing supports discrimination or exclusion but integration for better globalization. There will be a growing need for "thinking" about change, flexibility in strategy, and seeking opportunities.

Integrating the two approaches would be more effective, allowing us to perceive the solution and the benefit. In this sense, we must be an entrepreneur manager who thinks both in terms of solutions and opportunities. On the one hand, it helps to avoid the stalemate and not to get stuck. On the other hand, to take advantage and open new ways of development and progression before it is too late.

Finding opportunities should be as important as solving problems. They are the gateway to a professional career pivot. Once detected and grasped, they allow us to gain impetus and embark on our adventure.

c. Perception of Opportunity

What allows us to think in terms of opportunity and not just think in terms of problem-solving? It is the perception!

If we perceive the changes as problems to be solved, as the instability that threatens the implementation of the strategy, which thwarts our estimates, an obstacle to our development, our attention would be focused on the possible solution to a specific problem. However, solving a problem allows for maintaining the status quo, not development. In this sense, the vision is limited to solving problems to avoid or manage a deadlock situation. But is this enough to advance, develop, adapt, or even metamorphose in unstable and uncertain times?

Suppose we perceive change or uncertainty as opportunities that will allow us to experiment with new alternatives. In that case, we will focus on the benefit we can derive from such a change. Two key elements are used to assess an opportunity: feasibility and benefits.

The benefits: these are the benefits we will gain by seizing and creating a very special opportunity, and we especially know whether this benefit is worth the risks.

The feasibility: it is a question of whether an idea or a project can be put into practice, whether we have access to information and technology, and whether the economic and political conditions are favorable. Is the timing to our advantage?

d. The Attacker's Mindset: Offensive Approach

Uncertainty is part of our reality. It requires initiation to movement, taking the lead, approaching the possibilities preparing to arrive, and seizing the opportunities.

Thus, to be on the defensive in uncertain liquid times is, in other words, to refuse the changes that are ready to happen by laziness or by fear of hurting one's ego or not being able to succeed in future transitions.

It is up to you! Not taking the defensive is acknowledging the change and accepting the new reality. It is realizing that the skills you have no longer bring the desired added value. They are no longer in demand by the market and will potentially be an obstacle to development if they are not updated and enriched.

To be on the defensive is to remain stuck in one's place and be content to limit the damage while the biosphere moves and changes in its entirety. It is a form of intellectual and/ or mental passivity to protect what is already acquired and justify its stagnation by the failure of the education system, the lack of opportunities, by the economic and political conditions of the country, and to renounce any cognitive and intellectual responsibility that would allow us to reduce the gap and adjust to the market. People who are on the defensive are afraid to take risks and fear that they will not feel comfortable in the face of an unexpected event, new data, or even a new person. Gradually, they find themselves stuck and marginalized. They ignore the risk of not being part of the new rules of the game and prefer to stick to their convictions and acquired perceptions. Any new path involves taking risks and therefore making uncomfortable decisions inconsistent with our previous beliefs and perceptions. The greater the challenge, the greater the need for courage, a strong personality, self-knowledge, and a broad vision. Otherwise, we will be overwhelmed by events.

To be on the defensive is to sink into passivity without realizing it. To be on the offensive is to attack, to be in motion, continuity, and development. It means continuing to dance to the rhythm of change while learning new steps and keeping one's balance. This requires courage, risk-taking, and above all, a solid base of knowledge, an open mind, a well-developed perception, and flexibility.

To be on the offensive is to tackle opportunities, new ideas, and new challenges. It is to be constantly on standby.

Like the new technology, you should always download the new updates; otherwise, your device will "bugger" and no longer be in line with market demands. Like an attacker, you have to be confident and act, even if the vision is still ambiguous. Take the initiative and grasp the success factors of your project and create uncertainty for your competitor. We must succeed in seeing opportunity in all circumstances, in what is new and what is undergoing change. Playing the offensive does not mean being the first in what you do. The world did not change since the day technology was invented.

Each has his own timing to move; we must not rush into things and risk not doing them well, do not hang out and miss the opportunity. We are in liquid times where mobility and speed are important, but what ensures durability and persistence are solid foundations and agility. Giving time to opportunity means accepting changes that may occur along the way. The objectives are the same, but the way to achieve them and attack circumstances differs.

Thus, undertaking a new project and seizing an opportunity depends on three elements (Ram Charam, 2015):

1. The resources at your disposal.
2. Your assessment of the evolution, distortion, and trend of the market.
3. Your ability to resist, step back, and accept and manage failure.

To confidently attack, you have to see both sides of the same coin. To expect that the sanitary or economic crisis will pass and that the job offers will multiply is very optimistic. But the question to ask is, will you deal with the same markets? Will the industrialists make use of the same skills? Expecting what the market develops and for you to benefit from it without taking action is just a wish. You have to be mobile and active and try to formulate a holistic image so that you can prepare and act on time and not be out of phase. When you notice an anomaly, transformation, or simply a movement, do not ignore this perception. Do not run away but rather try to imagine a better scenario and method to take advantage of this future and probable transition.

In these times of uncertainty, to be on the defensive is to justify to ourselves the shortcomings and imperfections of our career and training. It is a lie to exonerate us. Such an attitude implies ignorance of oneself; little by little, you will no longer be adapted to the market's demands. It is necessary to adopt the routine of the attacker who continuously prepares, trains daily, experiments with new techniques, and learns new approaches. Therefore, on the day of the battle, he will manage to be reactive, to act quickly and effectively. This is why we need to be honest about the degree to which our skills are compatible with the demands and transformations of the potential market. Self-awareness and awareness of one's advantages and weaknesses is the first step in development and learning. By recognizing your weaknesses, you will know from whom you will ask for help and what service you are looking for to overcome your obstacles and dare change.

The illustration below shows that the passage from the change detection and identification phase to the research and design phase requires reflection and imagination. This results from the importance of the relationship between opportunity and the generation of ideas.

Imagining is putting aside instructions, judgments, beliefs, and rules and freeing your mind and thoughts. It is thinking abstractly without fearing the breadth of horizons.

Indeed, opportunity has a creative side; it requires visualization, imagination, dreams, freedom, and ambition. This creativity allows us to project ourselves into the future, build an image that is clear and ambiguous, and endow ourselves with the flexibility needed to adjust our strategy. Thus, an opportunity can be discovered, imagined, or created. The power of the imagination lies in its ability to give birth to new perceptions, ideas, and conceptions and improve and innovate what exists. To imagine is to dare the irrational and allow oneself to explore new paths and lands and to give oneself the opportunity to live one's dream of experiencing one's own path and realizing one's goals; it is an awareness of the power of imagination.

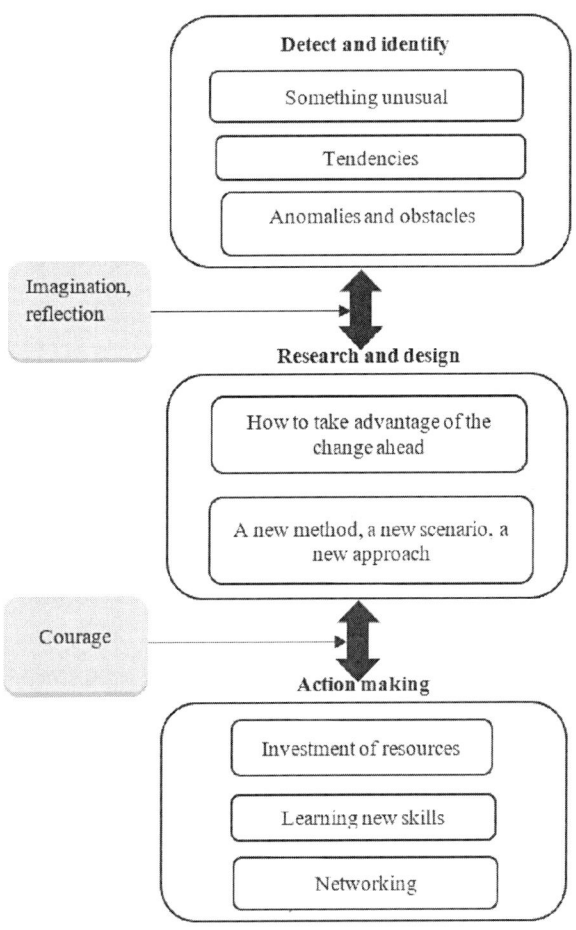

Figure 2: Attacking state of mind

The logic of the attacker does not follow a linear trajectory, just like liquid times. What counts is the useful learning and the success of the actions to be taken, regardless of the path. Uncertainty implies discovery and movement, not linearity.

The transition to a new path or way sets up quite special and particular challenges to be met. Nevertheless, never let yourself be discouraged or give up on your goals. Not everyone will believe in your vision. Have the courage to put your goals and beliefs in place and take the risks worth taking. Indeed, the challenges are there for you to learn more about and overcome them. That is how we learn and improve.

Moreover, surround yourself with experienced people who can bring you added value (advice, an opinion, a new perspective) and who actively listen and observe. Nothing is worth a rich and constructive network. Thus, the attack is no longer optional. In this world of prosperity and development in uncertainty, to be content with defense means decline: the loss of means and the limitation of skills. Dare to change, do not fear misappropriation, and remember that a change of direction can lead to a new offshoot; hence, the importance of flexibility and movement. Dance, the more steps you learn, the more you move freely on stage. You will fill the space and find the partner that best suits your movements.

2. Creation of Opportunities

"Luck favors only prepared minds," Pasteur said. We must be open to learning, adapting, and changing our thoughts, ideas, assumptions, beliefs, and behaviors. We cannot deny the major role that luck can play in the involvement of things and the establishment of favorable conditions to seize the opportunity and for success to take place. However, most importantly, this can only be achieved if you are prepared in advance. Create the conditions that will foster the emergence and development of opportunity. It is in this sense that opportunity becomes a chance. Do not forget that we are in liquid times and that the appearance of this opportunity alone does not allow us to go far. We must always think in terms of continuity and development. Indeed, creating and building opportunities is a call to change that must be prepared for. This change implies a distortion of what exists and can be accompanied by a feeling of fear, anxiety, and uncertainty. But once we are aware of the steps taken to seize and create the opportunity, adjust our strategy, and achieve our objectives, we will be able to cope with this feeling and no longer fear instability but rather try to understand it to take advantage of it.

The creation of opportunity requires:

a. Dynamic, Positive, and Committed Mindset

A state of mind that does not fear what is new or unusual but embraces uncertainties, detects changes, manages obstacles, and takes advantage of circumstances. Do not be a prisoner of acquired beliefs and judgments but be open to exploration and discovery. Do not be afraid to conceive of new ways or take a different view that does not conform with the rest of the world. Allow oneself to ask questions and accept differences. Accepting them does not mean adopting them but taking advantage of diversification and differentiation. By taking a different look and highlighting the gaps, we can open new horizons and create new opportunities.

In fact, our successes, failures, experiences, and beliefs are all filters that intervene in our perceptions and decisions and, therefore, in filtering opportunities. If our environment is changing and growing, so should our mindset.

Having a determined and positive mindset means learning from the efforts made, the failures experienced, and the experiences of others, which allows for a broader vision and an ability to transform obstacles into opportunities and turn negativity into positivity.

We must be aware of the filters that discard the various alternatives that do not conform to our reality and our roadmap to multiply and increase our chances of success. It is in this sense that opportunity is subjective. The more we are endowed with an open mindset, free from the various filters, that is dynamic, which operates in terms of alternatives and not in terms of binary logic, positive, that perceives both the momentary solutions and the horizons of development and improvement, the more we will be able to turn luck into an opportunity.

b. A Good Self-Knowledge

If we do not love ourselves, it will be hard to give love to others. Similarly, if we do not know ourselves, how can we distinguish between risks and opportunities? Self-knowledge is the first step to take to move forward with a safe step because achieving objectives requires both action and existence. To exist, one must have one's own personality, entity, and status.

To know oneself is to be aware of the strong and weak points. It is to choose who we want to be. It is to take our destiny into our hands and act instead of being subjected. Self-knowledge allows us to identify what is best for us, what is right for us, and what is right for our skills, experiences, and goals. This allows us to begin our journey and to detect the opportunities that allow us to develop and follow our vision. This is how we can set up our own path, not limit ourselves to following and melting into the flow. Knowing yourself makes it easier (Moore, 2021):

- Know what you want;
- Identify the final objectives you want to achieve;
- Determine what you need to be;
- Determine what you need to do;
- Get what you want.

Self-awareness helps to better prepare for opportunities and development in general. By knowing ourselves, we develop skills that go in the same direction as our goals and vision. Once the opportunity appears, we will be ready, not surprised, and be there at the right time to seize it. We will be lucky. That is when luck and chance will smile at us.

In uncertain liquid times, it is not only circumstances that change. We can and sometimes must change to achieve our goals and develop and become a better version that adapts to the uncertain nature of our reality. In fact, external factors are not always under control; it is impossible to control an economic crisis or stop the spread of an epidemic at a specific time. We cannot control the market's tendency to ask for specific skills. Nevertheless, we can control, develop and adjust ourselves. As long as we have an active mindset, every time a change occurs, we can master the information and knowledge we have, learn from uncertainties, and change accordingly. This is how we will be at the same time authentic, flexible, and true to ourselves. We develop our identity; we create ourselves and are reborn with each change.

c. Being Open to Learning

Openness to learning is an attitude anyone passionate about development and improvement holds. The people who seem to seize more opportunities and who seem to be lucky are the ones who take risks, try new things, put in more effort, and persevere more. They are open to change and are not limited to what is grasped but always keep an eye on developments and market trends. They are not afraid to step out of their comfort zone but rather look for ways and tools to succeed in their changes and adaptations. This is flexibility in thinking, perception, and behavior to stay in tune with market developments. It is about the willingness to learn for the sake of learning, not to graduate or get a job, but rather to evolve, keep pace with change, and embrace uncertainty. The most important thing is persistence and flexibility! This implies continuity, fluidity, and complementarity in acquired skills and knowledge. Learning new things makes us new people and allows us to get to know new people, make new connections, visit and explore new places, integrate new communities, and seize new opportunities.

Indeed, everything around us can be a source of learning, whether it is an event (the organization…), a television series (the decoration, the design of the furniture…), or the experience of a friend. Just perceive the element that would be useful to you, free you from judgments, and offer you the opportunity to contemplate difference, appreciate changes, and enjoy discovery.

- **Learn from new technology.**

We are in the age of new technology, so we might enjoy its advantages! We can seize this opportunity and learn about free online courses (Coursera, Udemy). You can watch videos on YouTube. The most important thing is choosing content that allows you to develop your skills and converges with your interests. Subscribe to Instagram accounts whose content is constructive and brings you added value. Be part of the communities that reflect your orientations, exchange ideas through comments and posts, and stay open to different opinions and suggestions. The Ted Talk also allows you to discover how speakers approach one subject or another, highlighting the diversity of approaches, gestures, smiles, looks, movement on stage, and interaction with the audience. Just one video of Ted Talk lets you learn at different levels.

- **Learn from others**

Try to learn from the people you see and meet when opportunity knocks. Asking for advice allows you to have external perspectives different from yours. Ask substantive questions, the answer to which enrich your knowledge, broaden your learning, develop your perception and above all, show the openness of your state of mind and reflect your curiosity and interest. Sometimes a sentence, word, or remark from the right person is enough to enlighten your vision, adjust your strategy, and take action. Share your plans and directions intelligently with the right people, the right profiles, and the ones you can learn from. Identify the keywords, formulate a concise and open-ended question, then seek their feedback and actively listen to the elements of their answers. This will allow you to steer the discussion in one direction or another, and do not forget that you do not necessarily share the same story, experiences, or beliefs. So have an open mindset to perceive what you are missing.

- **Learn from reading**

We do not only read for the pleasure of reading but also to learn. Whether it is a novel, a magazine, a personal development book, or a textbook, they are all sources of learning. We must choose the readings that enrich our knowledge, improve our skills, broaden our perceptions, introduce us to reflection, and motivate us.

d. Developing One's Visibility and Networking

Visibility is a key factor in creating opportunities. It is your visibility to others that will give rise to your existence. Put yourself in the right place and at the right time. Be careful not to be "in the middle of nowhere." Indeed, visibility offers us the advantage of connecting with people, sometimes without realizing it. It helps expand our network, which opens new doors and initiates new paths. Take part in events and actions, share your opinions and experiences on social networks, meet people, take initiative, and do new things. Have confidence in yourself, approach the people you meet, ask questions, and show your interest in their profiles, careers, and successes. This will allow you to establish relationships and improve your visibility, credibility, and network.

> **Visibility = credibility + connections**

An increase in visibility implies increased opportunities but also more criticism, rejection, and distressing energy. Do not be discouraged or hindered by such waves; do not take them personally. Perceive them as feedback and as information to be analyzed and processed in depth to convert them into opportunities and conceive of new ideas, new approaches, and not obstacles hindering your development.

3. Seizing the Opportunities

To think in terms of opportunities is to perceive the potential in what we encounter, whether it is ideas, people, circumstances, events, new technologies, or new concepts. It is seeing what others cannot visualize yet. What makes it possible to put such a state of mind in place is the ability to free oneself from judgments, equip oneself with flexibility, and be passionate, interested, and positive. Suppose some people are ahead of others in seizing opportunities. In that case, it is because they can look at things from different angles. They are not afraid of error or failure but accept themselves and are prepared for change. To seize it, we must look for it and identify it. But what is the difference? What is certain is that in both cases, you have to be prepared and open-minded.

a. Looking for Opportunities

The search for opportunities implies perseverance, experimentation, and process adjustment. It requires more mental and cognitive effort than identifying opportunities. It is about trying several times to open different doors until it works. You manage to seize the opportunity without underestimating the new market circumstances to be well prepared for the changes that may arise and not lose your flexibility and mobility.

It is not a matter of cloning or blindly copying successful projects and ideas but rather of adding value, distinguishing and reproducing them more cheaply, in better quality, with more options and better handling. You can learn from them and build a path matching your profile, skills, training, and environment. This is the safest and least risky type of opportunity, especially if you know how to add value to what exists.

It is about thinking about the skills you have, the means at your disposal, and how you can adjust and combine them to look for the opportunity in the right place from the right community and the right network. Otherwise, the downfall will be rapid, and the collapse will be probable and simple. Because you will not be armed with the tools, the techniques allow you to manage instabilities and changes.

In seeking out opportunities, we must be aware that we are not alone in doing so. This is what grants more value to the time factor and the accuracy of the search.

It is necessary to have a vision. Searching is not done arbitrarily or blindly but according to your logic, perception, and vision. This will allow you to make your way and succeed in your business, your professional career, or anything you undertake. In fact, each project, person, success, and experience has its own history, specificities, peculiarities, and biography. Therefore, reproducing what has already been done without any added value is not the best approach to ensure your project's continuity, flexibility, and development. We simply do not all share the same path of development. What corresponds to one may not correspond to the other. In this sense, in the search for opportunity, everyone must determine the pace that suits him and the market he wishes to approach while always having in mind "the big picture": an overview.

Finally, we must seek integration. Even when we think of opportunity, we must not exclude one perspective for the benefit of another. We must be able to include them all in our reflections and actions. Being on stand-by and identifying opportunities save time and takes the lead. However, this will only grow and prosper when we are open to continuous learning, allowing us to build and implement the opportunity. Suppose our perception is not as sharp, broad, and profound, and our observation is not well developed. In that case, it does not mean we will be unable to seize or identify a new opportunity. Still, by continually searching, we will be able to identify and build opportunity, to seize it. Everything is interconnected and interdependent, even when it comes to opportunities.

b. Identifying Opportunities

To spot is to identify and recognize an element or a situation...that is difficult to detect or when we try to detect. This depends on different factors such as our perceptions, profile (personality, flexibility and mobility, interests and passions), training (skills, knowledge, area of expertise), visions, and objectives.

Identifying opportunity requires certain pragmatism because we have to go straight to the point, have clarity in the ideas to know what we are trying to look for, and have the speed so that we take the lead and not be out of phase. It is also necessary to acquire a perceptive acuity to observe situations and events that arise in a well-developed way. Sometimes it is still early to determine precisely which opportunity best suits one's pursuit.

At this point, we must not get lost, be afraid or flee from this ambiguity, always remember that non-clarity can bring new alternatives and possibilities. Stand by and look out for the different opportunities on your way and, therefore, for the different ideas and possibilities that will rise to the surface and pass through your mind. But at this level, we must pay attention to an important point: the identification of opportunity can involve waiting and passivity, which does not suit our environment's liquid and uncertain nature. Staying in one's place, waiting for an opportunity to appear, is not always the best decision. It can make us an opportunist person, in the sense that the only effort made is limited to treasure hunting, without any effort for improvement or exploration. As soon as the opportunity arises, we seize it without taking into consideration the other side of the coin and without asking ourselves questions about continuity and development. It is rather momentary, and in this sense, the opportunity takes the form of a solution to a problem and is no longer an advantage to be grasped and developed. So when you spot an opportunity, it would be interesting to ask yourself:

- What are you going to learn?
- What skill will you develop?
- What are the development horizons?

Identifying opportunity requires maintaining an equal exchange with the environment around us, an exchange that saves both sides, whether a professional, friendly, or family relationship. For example, in a friendly relationship, an equal exchange can be represented by a friend who shares an experience, and the other brings a new version to his approach and a new perception of circumstances. This exchange allows both parties to enrich themselves and create added value. In fact, creating value makes your position stronger and gives you more value and credibility. Mutual exchanges will allow you to benefit and learn from each other and add value. Always be active and dynamic. On the other hand, a mutual exchange is not opportunism in the negative sense but rather a healthy relationship that pushes both sides forward, if not complete them. Neither party loses. Neither party negatively consumes the energy of the other but, instead, creates value mutually, attracting opportunities and broadening perceptions.

The sharpness of perception and the mutual exchange will help you save time, reduce ambiguity and identify your interests. There is nothing wrong with identifying opportunities, but it would be more interesting if it were accompanied by a research effort.

References

Bauman Z. (2007). *Liquid times: Living in an age of uncertainty*. Cambridge CB2 1UR, UK.

Bauman Z. (2000). *Liquid modernity*. Cambridge CB2 1UR, UK.

Bauman Z. and May T. (2019). *Thinking sociologically*. Wiley Blackwell.

Blake J. (2016). Pivot: the only move that matters is your next one. Penguin Random House, UK.

Castells, M. (2000). "Materials for an exploratory theory of the network society." *British Journal of Sociology Vol. No. 51 Issue No. 1* (January/March 2000) pp. 5–24 [http://www.tandf.co.uk/journals]. Fig.1 Photograph: Keystone/GettyImages: *http://folksonomy.co/?permalink=3877*

Castells M. (2010). *The information age: economy, society and culture*. Blackwell, Oxford, UK.

Castells M. and Cardoso G. (2005). The network society: from knowledge to policy. Center for transatlantic relations. Washington.

Charan R. (2015). The attacker's advantage: Turning uncertainty into breakthrough opportunities. Public Affairs, NY.

De Bono E. (2018). *Handbook for a positive revolution: the five success principles for personal and global change.* Vermilion, London.

De Bono E. (2017). *Practical thinking.* Vermilion, London.

De Bono E. (2017). *Atlas of management thinking.* Penguin Random House, UK.

De Bono E. (2015). *Serious creativity: How to be creative under pressure and turn ideas into action.* Penguin Random House, UK.

De Bono E. (2009). *Think before it's too late.* Penguin Random House, UK.

De Bono E. (1995). *Teach yourself to think.* Penguin Random House, UK.

De Bono E. (1994). *Future positive.* Penguin Random House, UK.

De Bono E. (1992). *I am right you are wrong*. Penguin Random House, UK.

De Bono E. (1991). *Handbook for a positive revolution: The five success principles for personal and global change.* Vermilion, London.

De Bono E. (2003). *Tactics: The art and science of success*. Profile books LTD, London.

Hasson G. (2021). *Career finder: where to go from here for a successful future*. Capstone.

Mathur A. and Pater R. (2019). *Safety leadership during uncertain times*. Ass.org May 2019 PSJ Professional safety. Maxwell J.C. (2009). *How successful people think*. Center street, Hachette Book Group, NY.

Ries E. (2017). The lean startup: How today's entrepreneurs use continuous innovation to create radically successful business. Currency International Edition. US.

Rob M. (2021). Opportunity: seize the day. Win at life. John Murray Press. Carmelite House. London EC4Y 0DZ.

Schwartz D. J. (2016). *The magic of thinking big*. Penguin Random House, UK.

Shafak E. (2020). How to stay sane in age of division. Profile Books LTD, London.

Smeets P. J. A. M. (2011). *Expedition Agroparks. Research by design into sustainable development and agriculture in the network society.* Wageningen Academic Publishers, the Netherlands.

Spinuzzi C. (2012). International advances in writing research: Culture, Places Measures. CHAPTER 27: Genre and generic labor. The WAC Clearinghouse.

Syrett M. and Devine M. (2012). Managing uncertainty: strategies for surviving and thriving in turbulent times. *The economist newspaper Ltd*, 2012.

Templar R. (2019). *The rules of thinking.* Pearson Education Limited, UK.

Tracy B. (2015). Creativity and problem solving. Library of Congress Cataloging-in-Publication data, USA.

Vernon M. (2010). *Understand humanism.* Library of Congress Catalogue, UK.

Whitmore S. J. (2017). Coaching for performance: The principles and practice of coaching and leadership. Fifth Edition. Nicholas Brealey Publishing, London.

https://www.oxfam.org.uk/education/who-we-are/what-is-global-citizenship/